GAMORA

GUARDIAN OF THE GALAXY

JIM STARLIN
WRITER & PENCILER

JIM STARLIN, AL MILGROM, STEVE LEIALOHA & JOSEF RUBINSTEIN WITH ALAN WEISS
INKERS

JIM STARLIN, MICHELE WOLFMAN & PETRA GOLDBERG
COLORISTS

TOM ORZECHOWSKI & ANNETTE KAWECKI
LETTERERS

LEN WEIN, MARV WOLFMAN & ARCHIE GOODWIN
EDITORS

J. SCOTT CAMPBELL & EDGAR DELGADO
FRONT COVER ARTISTS

JIM STARLIN
BACK COVER ARTIST

MARK D. BEAZLEY
COLLECTION EDITOR
SARAH BRUNSTAD
ASSOCIATE EDITOR
JOE HOCHSTEIN
ASSOCIATE MANAGER, DIGITAL ASSETS
CORY SEDLMEIER
MASTERWORKS EDITOR
JENNIFER GRÜNWALD
SENIOR EDITOR, SPECIAL PROJECTS

JEFF YOUNGQUIST
VP, PRODUCTION & SPECIAL PROJECTS
JEPH YORK
RESEARCH & LAYOUT
JAY BOWEN
BOOK DESIGNER
DAVID GABRIEL
SVP PRINT, SALES & MARKETING

AXEL ALONSO
EDITOR IN CHIEF
JOE QUESADA
CHIEF CREATIVE OFFICER
DAN BUCKLEY
PUBLISHER
ALAN FINE
EXECUTIVE PRODUCER

GAMORA: GUARDIAN OF THE GALAXY. Contains material originally published in magazine form as STRANGE TALES #180-181, WARLOCK #9-11 and #15, AVENGERS ANNUAL #7, and MARVEL TWO-IN-ONE ANNUAL #2. First printing 2016. ISBN# 978-1-302-90217-9. Published by MARVEL WORLDWIDE, INC., a subsidiary of MARVEL ENTERTAINMENT, LLC. OFFICE OF PUBLICATION: 135 West 50th Street, New York, NY 10020. **Printed in Canada.** ALAN FINE, President, Marvel Entertainment; DAN BUCKLEY, President, TV, Publishing & Brand Management; JOE QUESADA, Chief Creative Officer; TOM BREVOORT, SVP of Publishing; DAVID BOGART, SVP of Business Affairs & Operations, Publishing & Partnership; C.B. CEBULSKI, VP of Brand Management & Development, Asia; DAVID GABRIEL, SVP of Sales & Marketing, Publishing; JEFF YOUNGQUIST, VP of Production & Special Projects; DAN CARR, Executive Director of Publishing Technology; ALEX MORALES, Director of Publishing Operations; SUSAN CRESPI, Production Manager; STAN LEE, Chairman Emeritus. For information regarding advertising in Marvel Comics or on Marvel.com, please contact Vit DeBellis, Integrated Sales Manager, at vdebellis@marvel.com. For Marvel subscription inquiries, please call 888-511-5480. **Manufactured between 7/29/2016 and 9/5/2016 by SOLISCO PRINTERS, SCOTT, QC, CANADA.**

10 9 8 7 6 5 4 3 2 1

In *Strange Tales* #178-179, cosmic hero and Soul Gem wielder Adam Warlock encountered the fanatical, oppressive Universal Church of Truth — and Warlock was shocked to discover that the Magus, the Church's bloodthirsty "God," was somehow a reflection of Warlock himself! Now, allied with Pip the Troll, Warlock plans to unravel the mystery and defeat the Universal Church...

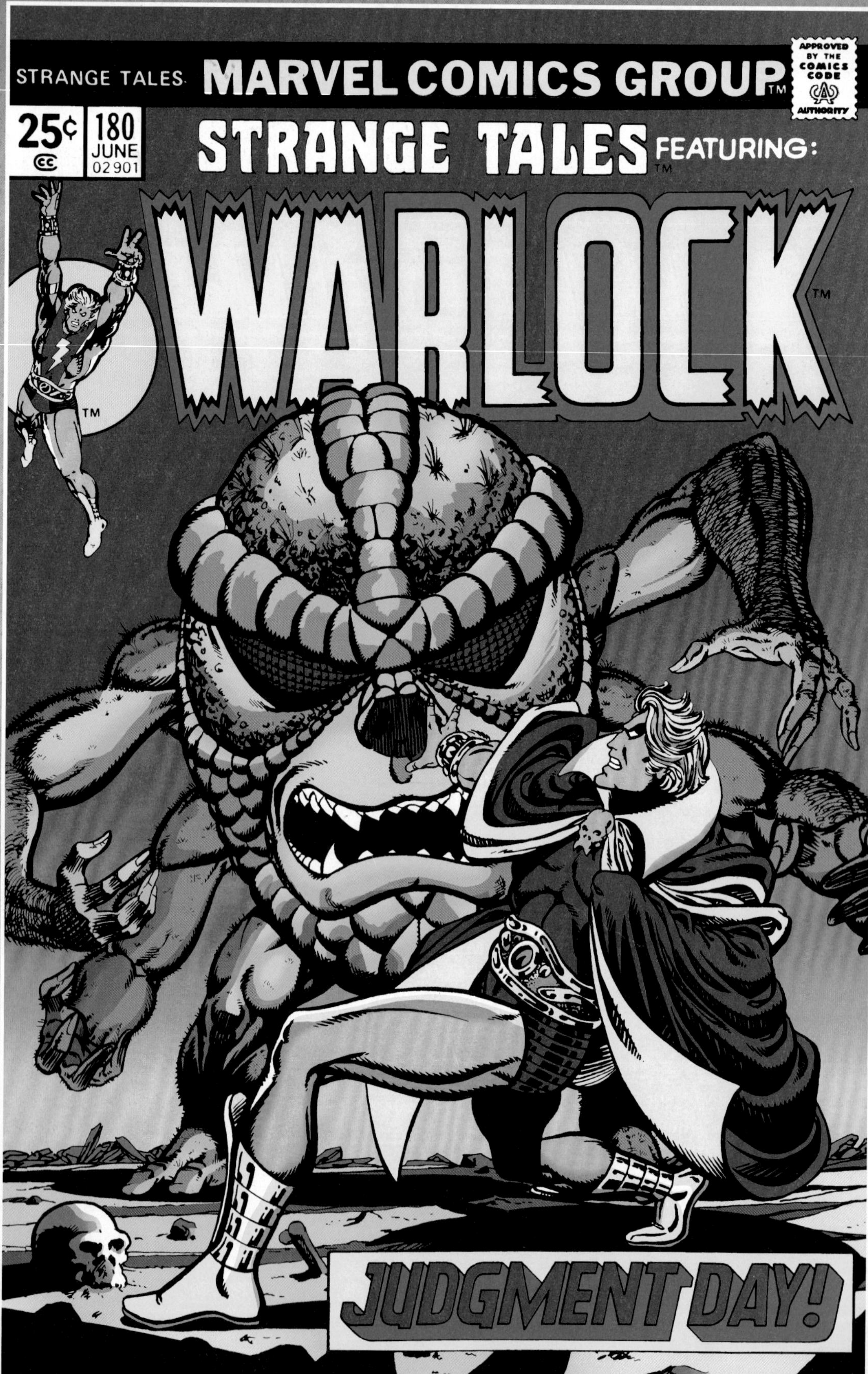

Born to be Earth's man of the future, then forced to abandon his native planet because of his alien ways, he wanders the stars seeking **LIFE**! Gifted with ultra-strength, paranormal reflexes and perceptions, the power of levitation and the curse of a vampire soul-gem, he stands uniquely **ALONE** among the heavens.

Stan Lee PRESENTS: **THE POWER OF WARLOCK!**™

STORY- SAM JILTIRN ART- JIM STARLIN INKS- J. L. MINIRATS
LETTERS- T. P. ORZECHOWSKI COLORS- MS. NATJIRIL EDITOR- LEN WEIN

FROM THE VERY **BEGINNING**, THE VOYAGE TO THIS CROSSROADS IN SPACE HAS BEEN LIBERALLY SPICED WITH **VIOLENCE** AND **DEATH!**

IT BEGAN WITH THE LOSS OF A YOUNG GIRL'S **LIFE!** SHE HAD COME TO **WARN** WARLOCK OF THE **MAGUS,** THE DEADLY GOD WORSHIPPED **BY THE UNIVERSAL CHURCH** OF **TRUTH!** ADAM WAS SOON TO LEARN THAT THIS FALSE DEITY WAS AND IS HIS OWN **OTHER SELF,** THOUGH HOW THIS CAN BE REMAINS A MYSTERY!

SETTING OUT TO ONCE AGAIN **CONFRONT** THIS DISINGENUOUS DIVINITY, WARLOCK SOON FOUND HIMSELF **CAPTIVE** ABOARD ONE OF THE UNIVERSAL CHURCH'S STARSHIPS, CONDEMNED TO DEATH BY THE **MATRIARCH,** THE RELIGION'S TEMPORAL LEADER!

THOUGH EASILY OVERCOMING THE SHIP'S **CREW,** ADAM NARROWLY AVOIDED DEATH AT THE HANDS OF **AUTOLYCUS,** THE STARSHIP'S CAPTAIN AND BLACK KNIGHT OF THE CHURCH! ONLY THE FACT THAT WARLOCK'S MYSTERIOUS **SOUL GEM** MOMENTARILY SPRANG TO INDEPENDENT LIFE AND STOLE THE CAPTAIN'S **SOUL,** SAVED THE ASTRAL AVENGER FROM CERTAIN DOOM!

UNFORTUNATELY, THIS RESCUE NEARLY **LOST** ADAM WARLOCK MORE THAN IT **GAINED,** FOR HE NOW MUST CARRY WITHIN HIMSELF THE MEMORY AND VERY SOUL OF HIS JEWEL'S **VICTIM!**

BUT FINALLY A SHIP'S **SHUTTLE CRAFT** WAS COMMANDEERED, AND SLIGHT ALTERATIONS WERE MADE ON ADAM'S COSTUME FOR SAKE OF ANONYMITY, AND THE LAST LEG OF THE JOURNEY HAS BEEN MADE IN THE COMPANY OF ONE PIP **THE TROLL,** A NEW-FOUND **ALLY** OF SORTS!

STILL, PIP SEEMS TO KNOW HIS WAY AROUND THIS WORLD BETTER THAN THE MEMORIES I STOLE FROM THE LATE AUTOLYCUS! POOR DEVIL!
BEST NOT TO DWELL ON THE GRISLY AFFAIR JUST YET! IT'S STILL TOO EARLY... TOO FRESH FOR MY SANITY TO ACCEPT...
... AND I'VE ALREADY ENOUGH DARK THOUGHTS TO DWELL UPON THIS DAY...
... SINCE I'VE COME TO THIS WORLD TO KILL A GOD!

HOW TO ACCOMPLISH THAT TASK SHOULD KEEP MY MIND SUFFICIENTLY OCCUPIED!
WHAT?!
OOOOF!

HEY!
WHY DON'T YOU WATCH WHERE YOU'RE GOING...

A TROLL!
A BLACK KNIGHT!

RAISE 'EM, TROLL-SCUM!
I FORGOT!
THE CHURCH HAS DECREED THAT ALL TROLLS SHOULD BE EXTERMINATED...

... BECAUSE OF THEIR "DEGENERATE WAYS"!
BUT I HAPPEN TO NEED THIS PARTICULAR DEGENERATE FOR THE MOMENT!

SO...
NICE SHOOTING, GOLDIE! LET'S SEE IF YOU CAN DO AS WELL...
KZAT!
... WITH THE FOUR KNIGHTS BEHIND YOU!
BY ORION! THAT TATTOOED TERROR HAS FRIENDS WITH HIM!

FOUR TRIGGER FINGERS TIGHTEN ON DEATH-DEALING LASERS!
THE RESPONSE: GOLDEN LIGHTNING AND CRIMSON AGONY!
HIS MOVEMENTS ARE GRACEFUL BUT DEVASTATING... PRECISE BUT MERCILESS, FOR HE KNOWS IT'S NO LONGER HIS LIFE ALONE AT STAKE!

HE BATTLES FOR THE FREEDOM OF A THOUSAND WORLDS! FOR SUCH STAKES ONE MUST BE UNSPARING!
THE MASSACRE IS OVER BEFORE IT HAS REALLY BEGUN!
'ATTA-BOY, DARK EYES!
PASTE HIM ONE FOR ME!

BOY, THEY SURE DON'T BUILD RELIGIOUS FANATICS LIKE THEY USED TO!
PIP... PLEASE SHUT UP!
IT'S THE... SOUL GEM... IT FIGHTS ME... IT'S TRYING TO... BREAK FREE... FROM MY CONTROL... AGAIN!

I CAN FEEL IT... IT WANTS TO SUCK IN... THE SOULS... OF THESE FALLEN KNIGHTS...
...JUST LIKE IT DID... TO AUTOLYCUS... I CAN'T ALLOW THIS... TO HAPPEN...
... NOT AGAIN!

I DID IT!
I'VE GOT IT UNDER CONTROL AGAIN!
BUT IT WAS SO...SO HARD!

I FEARED IT MIGHT COME TO THIS!
THE SOUL GEM IS STEADILY GROWING STRONGER AND SHEDDING THE SUBCONSCIOUS CONTROL I'VE HAD OVER IT THE LAST THREE YEARS!
IT SEEKS TO BE FREE TO SATISFY ITS UNHOLY HUNGER FOR FRESH SOULS, TO SUCK THEM OUT OF LIVING BEINGS!
I WEAR A FIEND UPON MY FOREHEAD... A MONSTER I NOW REALIZE...
...I MUST DESTROY!

TIME AND SPACE SHIFT! SHORT MINUTES LATER, MERE MILES AWAY:
YOUR MOST HOLINESS, THE MATRIARCH! I FEAR I MUST REPORT THAT THE INFIDEL, ADAM WARLOCK, HAS BEEN SIGHTED APPROACHING THE SACRED PALACE!
REALLY!

THESE ARE INDEED GLAD TIDINGS YOU BRING THIS DAY, PIOUS! I WAS AFRAID WE'D LOST DEAR ADAM!

I NEARLY MADE A SERIOUS MISTAKE EARLIER, TRYING TO HAVE WARLOCK KILLED! THAT MIGHT HAVE RUINED EVERYTHING!
FOR, IN WAYS NOT EVEN I UNDERSTAND, ALL THAT WE ARE AND ALL WE POSSESS DEPEND ON THIS STRANGE MAN!

IT'S FAR BETTER THAT HE LIVES TO SERVE ME THAN DIES AND DESTROYS ALL THAT I'VE BECOME!
SO BELIEVE ME WHEN I SAY... THAT IF ADAM WARLOCK IS FOOLISH ENOUGH TO COME TO THIS PALACE...
...HE'LL LEAVE HERE MY SLAVE!

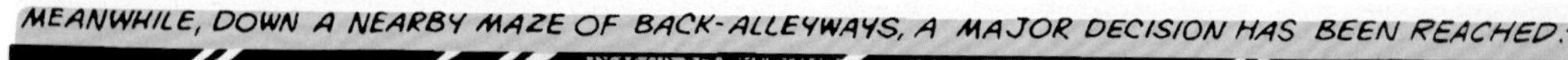
MEANWHILE, DOWN A NEARBY MAZE OF BACK-ALLEYWAYS, A MAJOR DECISION HAS BEEN REACHED!

THIS IS AS SECLUDED A PLACE AS ANY WE'LL FIND.
ONCE AGAIN, PIP, I ASK YOU TO LEAVE ME! WHAT I'M ABOUT TO DO MAY BE EXTREMELY DANGEROUS!
FORGET IT! THAT GEM WON'T BOTHER ME!
IT'D CHOKE ON MY SOUL!
VERY WELL!

THE TIME HAS COME FOR ME TO REMOVE THIS GEM -- THOUGH I'VE WORN IT SO LONG, IT ALMOST FEELS LIKE A PART OF ME!
IS THAT WHY MY FINGERS TREMBLE...

...AND A FEELING OF DOOM HANGS OVER ME?
YET, I AM MASTER OF THIS GEM!

I SHALL... URNK!

PAIN!! EMPTINESS!! IT FLOWS FROM ME... ALL THAT I WAS... AM... EVER WILL BE... GONE!
GONE!
GONE!
ADAM, WHAT'S WRONG?
HOLY BLUE RABIES!

MY GEM... MY LOVELY GEM...
THE GEM?! SURE! THAT MUST BE IT!
GOT TO PUT IT BACK!

OOOF!
BOY OH BOY, DID YOU SCARE THE BLANK OUT OF ME!
YOU OKAY NOW, GOLDIE?
NO, PIP!
I'M AFRAID I MAY NEVER BE ALL RIGHT... EVER AGAIN!

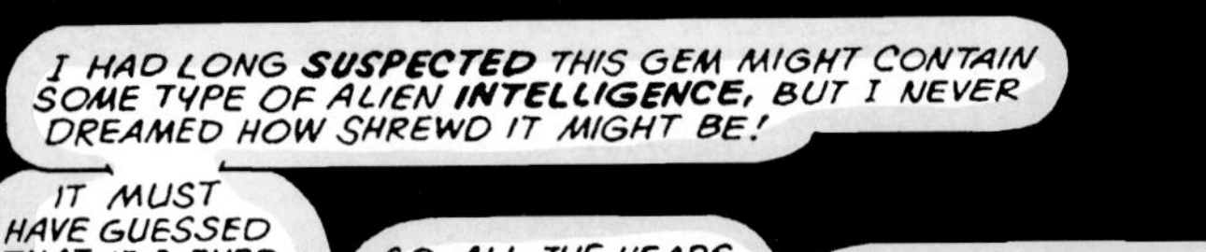
I HAD LONG SUSPECTED THIS GEM MIGHT CONTAIN SOME TYPE OF ALIEN INTELLIGENCE, BUT I NEVER DREAMED HOW SHREWD IT MIGHT BE!
IT MUST HAVE GUESSED THAT IF I EVER LEARNED OF ITS GHASTLY APPETITES, I WOULD DESTROY IT!
SO ALL THE YEARS I'VE WORN THIS GEM, IT'S BEEN SLOWLY AND SUBTLY SUCKING MY SOUL INTO ITSELF...
...UNTIL I AM NOTHING BUT A HOLLOW SHELL, DEPENDANT UPON IT FOR LIFE ITSELF!

SEPARATED FROM THE GEM, I AM LIKE A PUPPET WITH ITS STRINGS CUT!
IN OTHER WORDS, THAT GEM HAS BECOME MY LIFEFORCE AND I... ITS PRISONER!

SO... YOU'VE FINALLY DISCOVERED WHAT A MENACE YOU CARRY UPON YOUR BROW?
IT'S ONE OF THE MATRIARCH'S SPY SCANNERS!
LOOK! IT'S OLD 'SLINK' HERSELF!

I CAN READ THE QUESTIONS IN YOUR EYES, WARLOCK... AND THE ANSWER IS... YES!

YES, I KNEW YOUR SOUL GEM WOULD BECOME A MENACE EVEN BEFORE YOU REALIZED IT!
AS FOR HOW I KNEW...

...YOU'LL HAVE TO COME TO THE SACRED PALACE TO LEARN THAT SECRET!
SO UNTIL THEN...

STUFF IT, SLINK!
WHAT DOES SHE THINK WE ARE? IDIOTS?
WHAT AN OBVIOUS TRAP!
YES, OBVIOUS...

TRUE, THE BAIT WAS QUITE TEMPTING, BUT...
SAY, HOW DO YOU SUPPOSE SHE LEARNED ABOUT YOUR GEM?
I'VE NO IDEA!

WELL, WE'LL FIND OUT, BUT NOT BY WALKING INTO A DEATH TRAP!
RIGHT, ADAM?
ADAM?!

I HATED TO DESERT PIP IN SUCH A MANNER, BUT IT'S BEST THAT ONLY I FACE WHAT LIES AHEAD!
AFTER ALL, AM I NOT TO BLAME FOR ALL THE WRONG THAT HAS BEEN DONE? SO SHOULD NOT THE DANGER BE MINE ALONE?
IT'S MY SPIRIT THAT'S SUFFERING FROM A COSMIC DUAL PERSONALITY, THUS CREATING THE MAGUS!
IT'S MY RESPONSIBILITY TO FIND THE CURE!
BUT BEFORE ANYONE CAN CURE ANY DISEASE ONE MUST LEARN ITS CAUSE!
THOUGH I SUSPECT THAT THE MAGUS MIGHT BE ANOTHER CRUEL JEST ON THE PART OF MY SOUL GEM, I DARE NOT TAKE ANY ACTION AGAINST IT UNTIL I'M SURE!
I'M LIKE A MAN TRYING TO ASSEMBLE AN UNKNOWN PIECE OF MACHINERY IN THE DARK!
ONE WRONG MOVE ON MY PART MIGHT DESTROY ALL THE CAREFULLY BALANCED MECHANICS OF TIME AND SPACE...
...FOR I'M DEALING WITH THE HIGHLY DANGEROUS PROBLEM OF HAVING TWO IDENTICAL BEINGS LIVING IN THE SAME POINT OF WHEN AND WHERE!
MY ONLY HOPE IS THAT THE MATRIARCH MAY TRULY POSSESS SOME OF THE KNOWLEDGE I SEEK, FOR I NOW REALIZE THAT I'LL NEVER BE ABLE TO DEFEAT MY ENEMY IN A FRONTAL CONFRONTATION!
EVEN THOUGH WE MAY BE TWINS OF THE INNER SELF, IT'S OBVIOUS THAT THE MAGUS' PERSONAL STRENGTH FAR SURPASSES MY OWN!
THAT POWER, AUGMENTED BY A MILITARY FORCE OF THE UNIVERSAL CHURCH MAKES THE MAGUS A NEARLY IMPOSSIBLE FOE TO STOP!
YET STOP HIM I MUST!
FOR IF I FAIL, ALL LIFE FALLS WITH ME!
I'M SURE MY OTHER SELF WILL NEVER BE SATISFIED WITH ANYTHING LESS THAN TOTAL DOMINATION OVER ALL LIVING THINGS THROUGHOUT ALL SPACE...
...FOR, WOULD I DESIRE ANYTHING LESS IF I CHOSE HIS PATH?

FINALLY ARRIVING AT THE SACRED PALACE...
... WARLOCK FINDS IT NO PROBLEM TO AVOID THE...

... COLD, SEARCHING EYES OF THE PALACE GUARDS OR THE DULL ORBS OF THE FRONTALLY LOBOTOMIZED PALACE SERVANTS!

YOUR HOLINESS, THE INFIDEL HAS AGAIN BEEN SIGHTED NEARING THE PALACE!
SHALL I SUMMON YOUR PERSONAL GUARD?
NO, I'LL DEAL WITH THIS WARLOCK MYSELF!

THEN BEGIN DEALING, MADAM!
ADAM WARLOCK HAS ARRIVED!

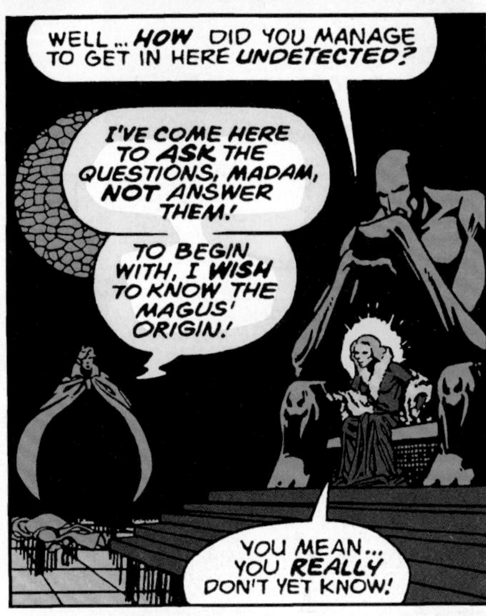
WELL ... HOW DID YOU MANAGE TO GET IN HERE UNDETECTED?
I'VE COME HERE TO ASK THE QUESTIONS, MADAM, NOT ANSWER THEM!
TO BEGIN WITH, I WISH TO KNOW THE MAGUS' ORIGIN!
YOU MEAN... YOU REALLY DON'T YET KNOW!

NOT DEFINITELY... THOUGH I STRONGLY SUSPECT MY SOUL GEM OF CREATING HIM!
SECONDLY, HOW DID YOU KNOW MY GEM HAD BEGUN TO REBEL AGAINST ME?

WELL, TO ANSWER YOUR SECOND QUESTION FIRST... THE MAGUS TOLD ME IT HAD HAPPENED A LONG TIME AGO!
A LONG TIME AGO...?
THAT'S RIGHT!

YOU SEE, YOUR SOUL GEM DID NOT CREATE THE MAGUS! YOU DID!
SURELY, YOU MUST SENSE WHAT I SAY IS TRUE! THE MAGUS IS NOT PART OF YOU... HE IS YOU...

...THE YOU OF THE FUTURE!

NO! THIS CAN'T BE TRUE!
I COULD NEVER BECOME THIS EVIL!
YOU SEEK TO TRICK ME!

LOOK AT YOURSELF, WARLOCK!
YOU'VE ALWAYS BEEN A CREATURE OF PASSION AND EXCESS!
YOU EITHER LOVE DEARLY OR HATE VICIOUSLY!
YOU'VE NO MIDDLE GROUND FOR YOUR EMOTIONS!
THAT'S YOUR OWN SPECIAL BRAND OF MADNESS AND THE REASON YOU'LL SOMEDAY...
...BECOME THE MAGUS YOURSELF!

NEVER! NOW THAT I KNOW, I'LL NOT ALLOW IT TO HAPPEN!
TRUE... IF ANYONE COULD CHANGE HIS OWN PREORDAINED FUTURE, IT WOULD BE YOU!
BUT YOU MIGHT ALSO CHANGE MY FUTURE...

...AND I'VE BECOME QUITE FOND OF RULING A THOUSAND WORLDS!
SO THAT'S WHY YOU'VE NOT ATTEMPTED TO KILL ME TODAY!

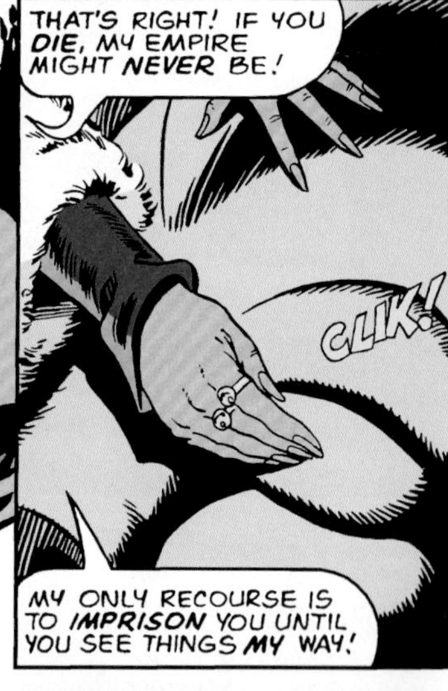
THAT'S RIGHT! IF YOU DIE, MY EMPIRE MIGHT NEVER BE!
CLIK!
MY ONLY RECOURSE IS TO IMPRISON YOU UNTIL YOU SEE THINGS MY WAY!

AND HOW DO YOU PLAN TO DO THAAAAAAAAAA
UNABLE TO CONCENTRATE QUICKLY ENOUGH TO LEVITATE...
... WARLOCK DROPS THROUGH THE HIDDEN TRAP DOOR...

... AND GRACEFULLY LANDS IN WHAT ADAM PRESUMES TO BE THE PALACE'S DUNGEON!

IMMEDIATELY, WARLOCK IS AWARE THAT HE IS NOT ALONE IN THIS BLACKNESS! FOR LONG DRAWN MOMENTS THE OMINOUS DARKNESS HANGS...
...THEN, ABRUPTLY, THERE IS LIGHT!

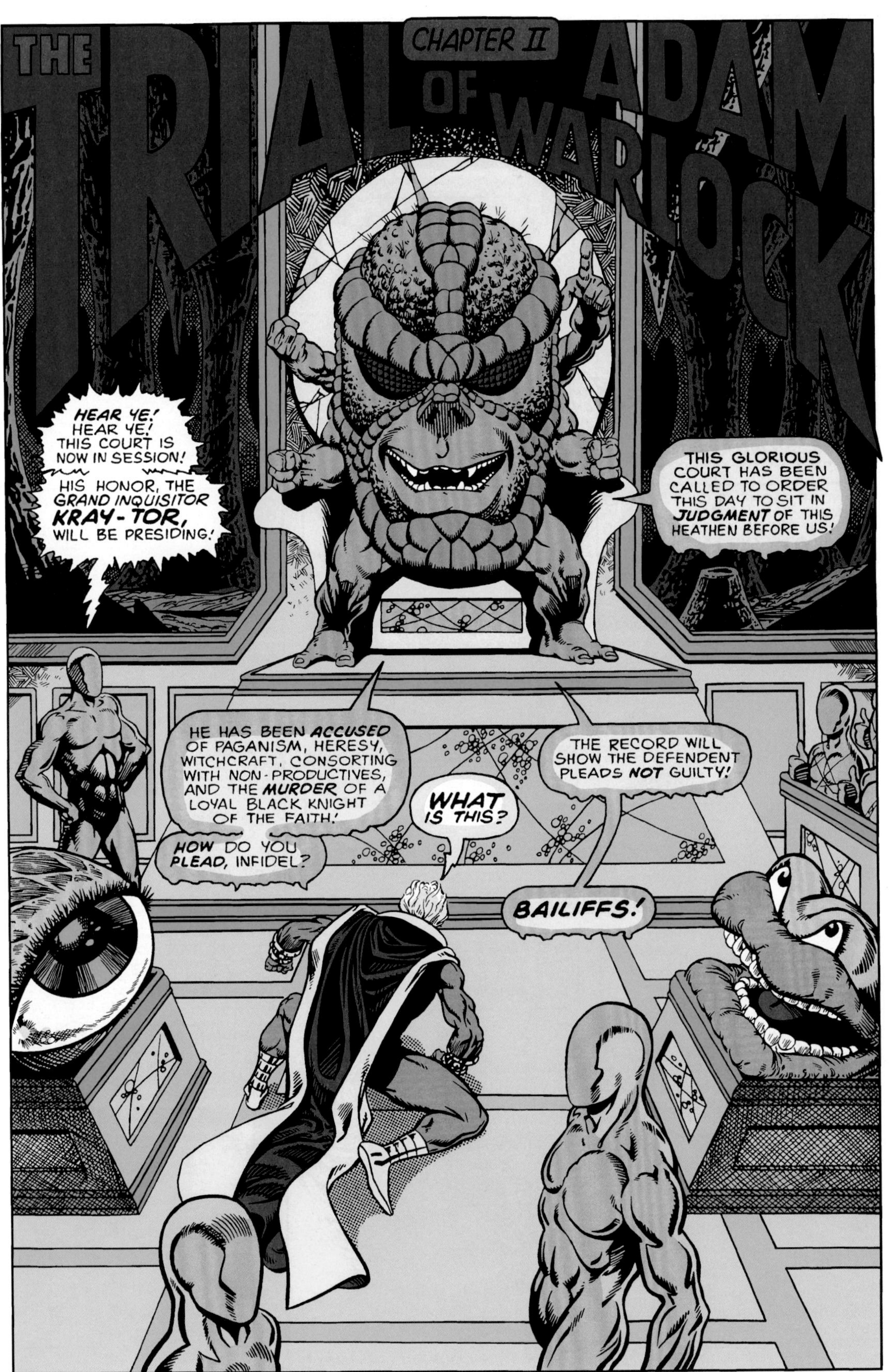
THE TRIAL OF ADAM WARLOCK
CHAPTER II
HEAR YE! HEAR YE! THIS COURT IS NOW IN SESSION!
HIS HONOR, THE GRAND INQUISITOR KRAY-TOR, WILL BE PRESIDING!
THIS GLORIOUS COURT HAS BEEN CALLED TO ORDER THIS DAY TO SIT IN JUDGMENT OF THIS HEATHEN BEFORE US!
HE HAS BEEN ACCUSED OF PAGANISM, HERESY, WITCHCRAFT, CONSORTING WITH NON-PRODUCTIVES, AND THE MURDER OF A LOYAL BLACK KNIGHT OF THE FAITH!
HOW DO YOU PLEAD, INFIDEL?
WHAT IS THIS?
THE RECORD WILL SHOW THE DEFENDENT PLEADS NOT GUILTY!
BAILIFFS!

RESTRAIN THE PRISONER!
HE HAS A HISTORY OF VIOLENCE!
I'LL NOT HAVE THIS COURT NEEDLESSLY INTERRUPTED!

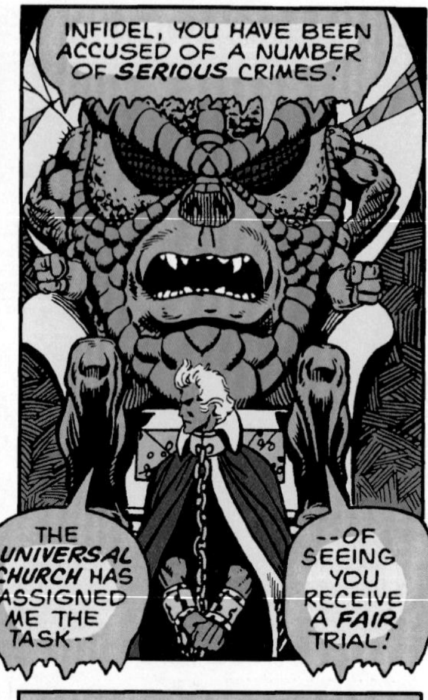
INFIDEL, YOU HAVE BEEN ACCUSED OF A NUMBER OF SERIOUS CRIMES!
THE UNIVERSAL CHURCH HAS ASSIGNED ME THE TASK--
--OF SEEING YOU RECEIVE A FAIR TRIAL!

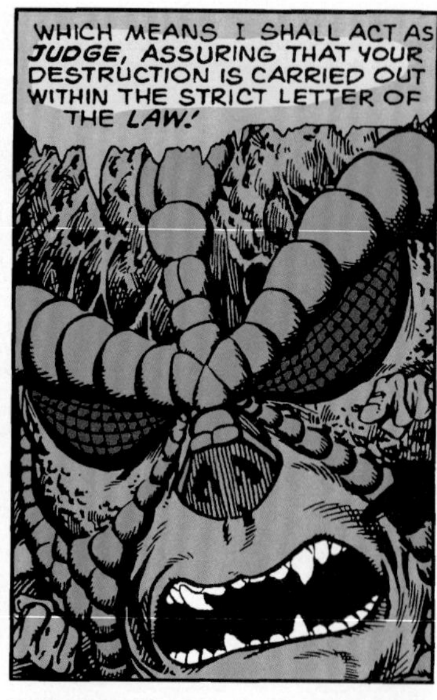
WHICH MEANS I SHALL ACT AS JUDGE, ASSURING THAT YOUR DESTRUCTION IS CARRIED OUT WITHIN THE STRICT LETTER OF THE LAW!

TO YOUR RIGHT IS OUR DISTRICT PROSECUTOR. HE SHALL SUPPLY US WITH PHONY CHARGES, LYING WITNESSES AND FALSIFIED EVIDENCE!

TO YOUR LEFT IS YOUR COURT-APPOINTED DEFENDER! HE'LL SUPPLY YOU WITH THE BEST LEGAL COUNCIL AVAIL-ABLE, IF HE CAN STAY AWAKE!

ONCE THE EVIDENCE OF YOUR GUILT HAS BEEN PROVEN, YOUR FATE WILL BE DECIDED...
...BY YONDER JURY OF YOUR PEERS!

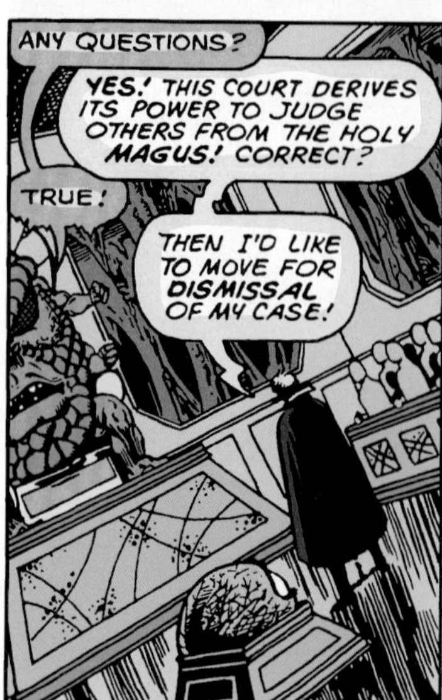
ANY QUESTIONS?
YES! THIS COURT DERIVES ITS POWER TO JUDGE OTHERS FROM THE HOLY MAGUS! CORRECT?
TRUE!
THEN I'D LIKE TO MOVE FOR DISMISSAL OF MY CASE!

THIS COURT IS QUITE AWARE THAT THE MAGUS AND I ARE ONE AND THE SAME BEING, THUS MAKING IT IMPOSSIBLE...
...FOR THIS COURT TO TRY ME!

YOUR POWER COMES FROM A PART OF ME GONE MAD! THIS MAKES YOU UNFIT AND UNQUALIFIED TO PASS JUDGMENT UPON ME!
I DEMAND TO BE TRIED BY THE MAGUS HIMSELF!

MOTION DENIED!
THE PRISONER WILL REFRAIN FROM ANY FURTHER OUTBURSTS OR FIND HIMSELF GASSED!

ANY MOTIONS OR OBJECTIONS WILL BE MADE BY YOUR PUBLIC DEFENDER! THAT'S HIS JOB!
BUT, HE HAS NO MOUTH!

I WARN YOU! THIS COURT HAS THE RESPONSIBILITY TO SHOW THE POPULACE THAT EVEN A FILTHY HEATHEN LIKE YOU WILL RECEIVE A FAIR TRIAL HERE!
SO EVEN THOUGH YOU AND I KNOW IT'S ALL A SHAM AND THAT YOUR FATE HAS AREADY BEEN DECIDED, YOU'D BEST PLAY ALONG WITH US!
DO YOU UNDERSTAND?

PERFECTLY!

THE PROSECUTION WILL CALL ITS FIRST WITNESS!
THE CHURCH WISHES TO CALL...

... YON-LOK, REBEL AND INFIDEL, TO THE STAND!
CITIZEN YON-LOK, WILL YOU POINT OUT...

...TO THIS COURT THE MAN YOU ACCUSE OF HIGH CHURCH CRIMES!
GLADLY!

HE'S THE ONE!
HE AND EVERY MEMBER OF THIS COURT!

I ACCUSE YOU ALL!

YOU'RE GUILTY OF TWISTING EVERYTHING THAT WAS GOOD UNTIL IT NOW SERVES NOTHING BUT YOUR OWN EVIL ENDS!
BAILIFFS!

SILENCE THE WITNESS!
THE JURY IS INSTRUCTED TO--

"--DISREGARD THIS WITNESS' TESTIMONY!"

SLOWLY THE TRIAL PROCEEDS! A STEADY FLOW OF EXPERTLY COACHED WITNESSES NOW UNERRINGLY POINT OUT WARLOCK AS THE PERPETRATOR OF A DOZEN FALSE CRIMES!

IN GRIM SILENCE ADAM WATCHES THE MAGUS' COMEDY OF JUSTICE NEAR ITS CLIMAX, UNTIL...
I... OBJECT!

IN FACT, I OBJECT TO EVERYTHING!
THIS COURT!
ITS LAWS!
ITS ETHICS!
ITS OFFICERS!
BUT MOSTLY ITS JUDGE!

THE PRISONER HAS BEEN WARNED REPEATEDLY TO REMAIN QUIET!
BAILIFFS, GAG HIM!

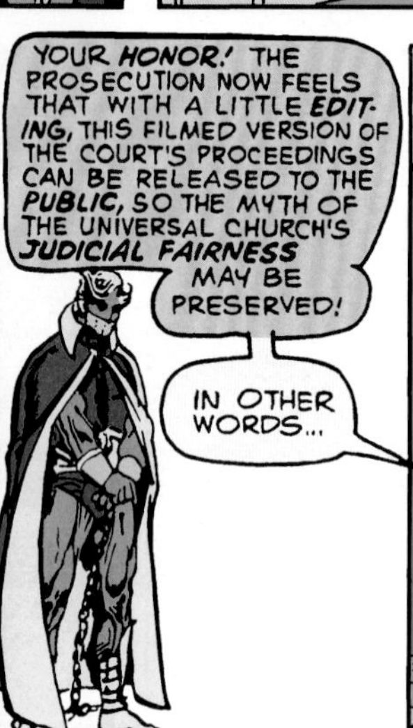
YOUR HONOR! THE PROSECUTION NOW FEELS THAT WITH A LITTLE EDITING, THIS FILMED VERSION OF THE COURT'S PROCEEDINGS CAN BE RELEASED TO THE PUBLIC, SO THE MYTH OF THE UNIVERSAL CHURCH'S JUDICIAL FAIRNESS MAY BE PRESERVED!
IN OTHER WORDS...

... THE CHURCH RESTS ITS CASE AND ASKS THIS COURT TO FIND THE DEFENDANT GUILTY!
GUILTY!
GUILTY!

HEARD AND HEEDED!
DOES THE DEFENSE HAVE ITS CLOSING STATEMENT READY AT THIS TIME?

THE RECORD WILL SHOW THE DEFENSE THREW ITSELF AT THE MERCY OF THE COURT!

THE TIME HAS COME TO DETERMINE YOUR GUILT OR INNOCENCE, INFIDEL!
JURY, MAKE YOUR DECISION!

GUILTY!

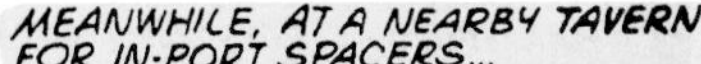
MEANWHILE, AT A NEARBY TAVERN FOR IN-PORT SPACERS...

BLAST THAT WARLOCK'S EYES, EARS, AND ANY OTHER ORGAN HE MIGHT HAVE USE FOR!
I'VE BEEN DESERTED!

HERE I LEAD HIM TO THIS JUNKHEAP PLANET FOR SOME EXCITEMENT, BUT AS SOON AS THINGS BEGIN TO GET INTER-ESTIN'.. I GET LEFT BEHIND!
BARKEEP! ONE MERDE STINGER-- HEAVY ON THE STING!

WELL, I REFUSE TO LET THIS RUIN MY STAY HERE ON HOME-WORLD, 'BIRTHPLACE OF THE ONE TRUE RELIGION'! MIGHT AS WELL DESECRATE ONE OF ITS TEMPLES WHILE I'M HERE!
THAT'LL BE FUN!

HEY YOU! TROLL! YOUR NAME PIP, BY ANY CHANCE?
WHAT'S IT TO YOU?
PLENTY! ALL THE CHURCH RADIO BANDS HAVE GOT AN 'ALL POINTS' OUT ON YOU...
... AND YOU PLAN TO TURN ME IN FOR THE REWARD?

KEEP YOUR HANDS ON THE BAR, MAGGOT, 'LESS YOU WANT THIS IN YOUR GUT!
BUT JUST TO SET YOUR MIND AT EASE, I'M NOT LOOKING TO COLLECT THE BOUNTY ON YOU!

IN FACT, I'M NOT INTERESTED IN YOU AT ALL, FLEA BAG!
I'M SEEKING YOUR FRIEND, ADAM WARLOCK!
WELL, I'M AFRAID YOU'RE A BIT TOO LATE, SISTER! WE'VE PARTED COMPANY!

HE RAN OFF TO THE SACRED PALACE AND LEFT ME BEHIND!
FOR ALL I KNOW, HE MIGHT BE DEAD BY NOW!
WHY ARE YOU LOOKING FOR HIM, ANYWAY?
I'VE COME TO SEE IF THIS WARLOCK REALLY HAS A CHANCE OF DEFEATING THE MAGUS!

IF HE DOES, I PLAN TO JOIN HIM!
IF HE DOESNT, I PLAN TO KILL ADAM WARLOCK!

ADAM WARLOCK, YOU HAVE BEEN FOUND GUILTY...
... AND ARE HEREBY SENTENCED TO A CHURCH-HOUSE OF CORRECTION!

'HOUSE OF CORRECTION'? MORE LIKE A BRAINWASHING CENTER, I'D SAY!

BAILIFFS, THE PRISONER'S SLIPPED HIS CHAIN! RESTRAIN HIM!
LAST TIME THESE SILVER-PLATED CRETINS GRABBED ME, I PLAYED ALONG WITH THEM!
I WANTED TO SEE FIRST HAND JUST HOW PERVERTED THE MAGUS' IDEA OF JUSTICE COULD TRULY BE!
WELL, NOW I KNOW...

...SO THESE COLD AND HEARTLESS ENFORCERS OF YOUR LAW CAN MEET THE FATE...
...THEY SO RICHLY DESERVED THE FIRST TIME THEY MANHANDLED AND BOUND ME!

I MIGHT ALSO TAKE THIS OPPORTUNITY TO EXPRESS THE CONTEMPT I FEEL...
...TOWARD THIS MINDLESS AND HEARTLESS 'JURY OF MY PEERS' AND THE REST OF THESE PROCEEDINGS!

NEVER HAVE I SEEN EVIL WEAR SUCH SANCTIMONIOUS ROBES!
YOU CLAIM TO BE JUSTICE, YET IN TRUTH YOU'RE NOTHING MORE THAN GLORIFIED SLAVE KEEPERS!

YOU ENFORCE LAWS THAT GRIND ANY WHO SEEK FREEDOM UNDER YOUR LEGAL HEELS!
THEN YOU FOOL THE GENERAL PUBLIC INTO THINKING THAT YOUR POLITICAL MURDERS...
... ARE THE ACT OF HEAVENLY JUSTICE!

WELL, I SEE YOUR VILLAINY FOR WHAT IT TRULY IS!
SO SPOUT NO GRAND PHRASES AS YOU SEEK TO DESTROY ME...
... FOR I'M SICK OF THIS GAME AND WILL PLAY NO LONGER!

VERY WELL, THEN!
SINCE YOU REFUSE TO SUBMIT TO CHURCH REHABILITATION, I AM FORCED TO REVERSE MY PREVIOUS, MERCIFUL, RULING AND SENTENCE YOU NOW TO...
...DEATH!

SO NOW, WITH THE POWERS VESTED WITHIN ME, I HEREBY DECREE THAT YOU SINK WITHIN THE MIRE OF YOUR OWN CRIMES!
THE FLOOR, YOU MEAN!

YES, BUT IT WILL BE THE WEIGHT OF YOUR OWN SINS WHICH PULLS YOU STEADILY DOWNWARD!
A PULL NOT EVEN MY SOUL GEM SEEMS CAPABLE OF REVERSING!

OF COURSE NOT, FOR IT IS THE POWER OF THE CHURCH WHICH BINDS YOU...
... THE POWER OF A RIGHTEOUS AND VENGEFUL GOD WHICH IS ABOUT TO DESTROY YOU!

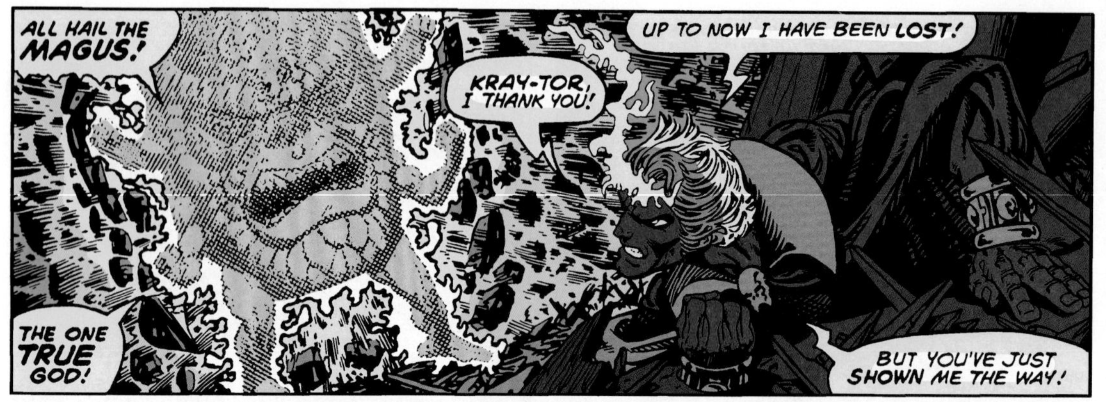

NO!

A FLAMING EMERALD BEAM FLASHES FROM THE SINISTER SOUL GEM AND KRAY-TOR'S SOUL IS WRENCHED FROM HIS BODY, AND FLOWS INTO THE FRENZIED ADAM WARLOCK!

"MEMORIES, IMAGES, THOUGHTS LIKE NONE I'VE EVER TASTED!

"DELICIOUS."

WHAT HAVE I DONE?
I'VE JUST ALLOWED... NO, COMMANDED THE GEM TO STEAL A SOUL!
WHAT'S COME OVER ME?

BUT CAN'T THINK OF THAT NOW... CAN'T THINK, PERIOD! SO MANY THOUGHTS IN MY HEAD... NOT MINE!
THEY'RE KRAY-TOR'S THOUGHTS... NO!

OH NO!
AT LAST I UNDERSTAND!
HE TRULY BELIEVED... WHAT HE DID ...WAS JUST!
I THREATENED HIS BELIEFS! IN HIS MIND... I WAS A VILLAIN!
EVEN WORSE YET... BY STEALING HIS SOUL...

...I PROVED HIM RIGHT... ooooh...

YES, YOU DO AT LAST UNDERSTAND! WE'RE ALL HEROES IN OUR OWN MINDS...

...EVEN ME!
BUT YOU'RE BEYOND CARING ABOUT SUCH THINGS, AREN'T YOU?
YOU PROBABLY DON'T EVEN CARE THAT I EXPECTED YOU TO PURLOIN THE JUDGE'S SPIRIT!
YOU SEE, ADAM, THAT WAS THE ONLY WAY I COULD THINK OF TO SAFELY RENDER YOU SENSELESS!

I COULDN'T TAKE THE CHANCE OF YOU BEING KILLED IN AN ARMED CONFRONTATION...

...AND I COULDN'T BRAINWASH YOU WHILE YOU REMAINED CONSCIOUS!

BUT, I'LL EXPLAIN ALL THIS TO YOU WHEN THE WORKERS IN THE PIT ARE THROUGH INDOCTRINATING YOU...
...I HOPE!

NEXT:
THE SECRET OF THE PIT... PIP TO THE RESCUE... AND...
1,000 CLOWNS

STRANGE TALES MARVEL COMICS GROUP

APPROVED BY THE COMICS CODE AUTHORITY

STRANGE TALES FEATURING:

WARLOCK

I WARNED YOU, WARLOCK!

THERE'S NO ESCAPE FROM THE...

STARLIN and WEISS 75

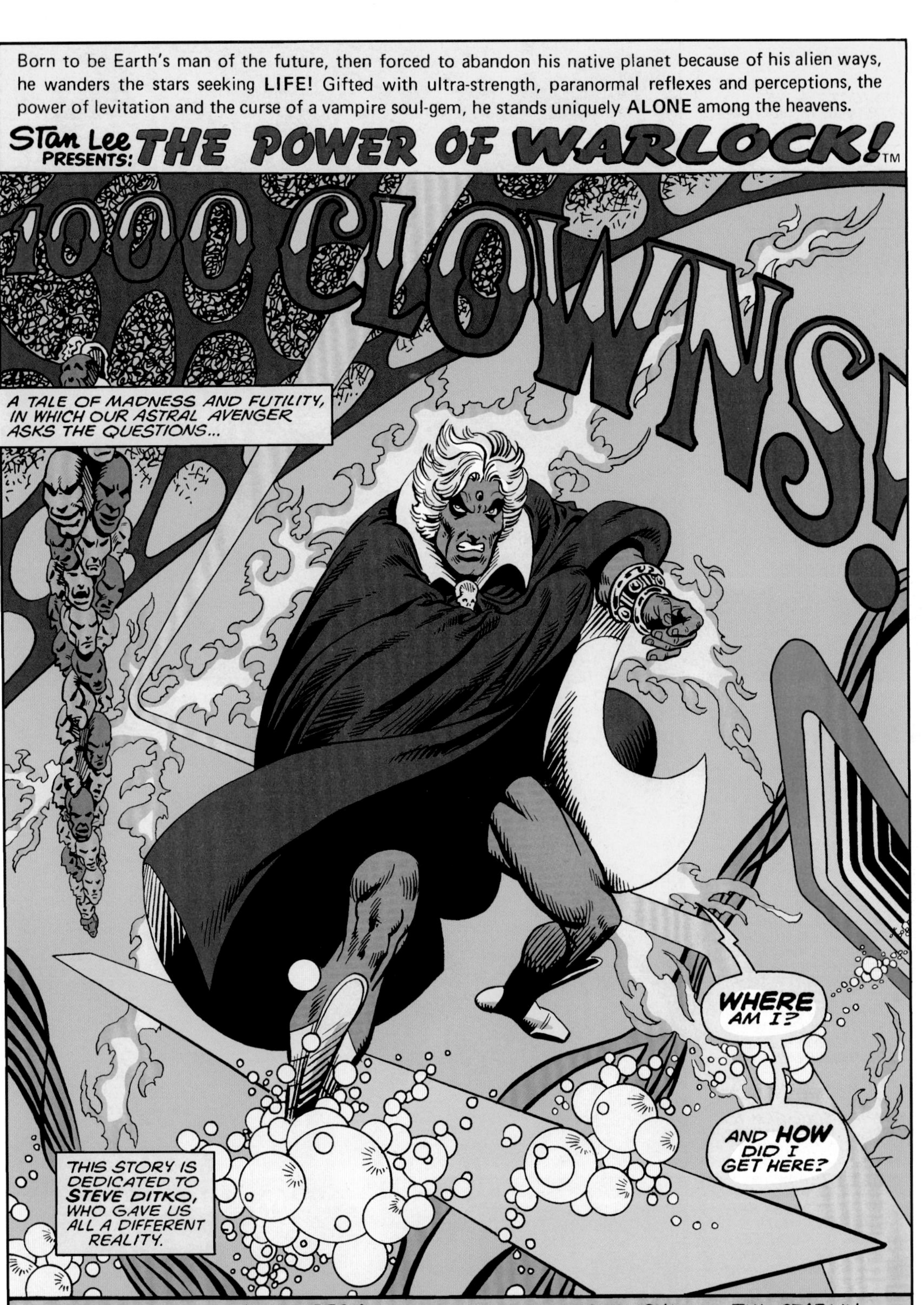
Born to be Earth's man of the future, then forced to abandon his native planet because of his alien ways, he wanders the stars seeking LIFE! Gifted with ultra-strength, paranormal reflexes and perceptions, the power of levitation and the curse of a vampire soul-gem, he stands uniquely ALONE among the heavens.
Stan Lee PRESENTS: THE POWER OF WARLOCK! TM
1000 CLOWNS!
A TALE OF MADNESS AND FUTILITY, IN WHICH OUR ASTRAL AVENGER ASKS THE QUESTIONS...
WHERE AM I?
AND HOW DID I GET HERE?
THIS STORY IS DEDICATED TO STEVE DITKO, WHO GAVE US ALL A DIFFERENT REALITY.
LEN WEIN EDITING • AL MILGROM INKING • TOM ORZECHOWSKI LETTERING • JIM STARLIN INSANITY

WELL, ADAM, IT APPEARS **NONE** OF THE FREE-FLOATING INANIMATE OBJECTS IN THIS STRANGE WORLD ARE GOING TO **ANSWER** YOU! SO...

...IT'S ONCE AGAIN UP TO **YOU** TO INVENT YOUR OWN **EXPLANATIONS!** REVIEWING THE **PAST** MAY POSSIBLY SHED SOME LIGHT ON MY **PRESENT** SITUATION!

AS I RECALL, I HAD FINALLY CONFRONTED THE **MATRIARCH**, THE TEMPORAL LEADER OF THE INSIDIOUS **UNIVERSAL CHURCH OF TRUTH!** THIS BLACK RELIGION WORSHIPS THE **MAGUS**, MY SINISTER OTHER SELF, AND THE TRUE POWER BEHIND THE MATRIARCH'S REIGN OF TERROR!

I HAD BEEN FOOLISH ENOUGH TO BELIEVE I MIGHT **TERRORIZE** MUCH-NEEDED INFORMATION ABOUT MY **ALTER EGO** FROM THE MATRIARCH, BUT THE CLEVER WOMAN-PRIEST TURNED THE TABLES ON ME BY SETTING ONE OF HER **CREATURES** UPON ME!

I WAS FINALLY FORCED TO USE MY VAMPIRE **SOUL-GEM** TO DEFEAT THE MONSTER, NOT REALIZING THAT ABSORBING ITS **SOUL** INTO MYSELF WOULD BE **TOO MUCH** FOR MY FRAIL MIND TO ACCEPT! THE MONSTROSITY'S **THOUGHTS AND FEELINGS** WERE SO ALIEN, I HAD TO ESCAPE INTO OBLIVION TO SAVE MY **SANITY!**

BUT I NOW **REALIZE** THAT AS THE **LAST BITS** OF REALITY FLED FROM MY CONSCIOUSNESS, I FELT COLD INHUMAN HANDS GRIP ME AND **DROP** ME INTO A NEARBY PIT!

"YET **HOW** I CAME TO WHEREVER I AM NOW REMAINS A **MYSTERY!**"

'HERE' MAY ONLY BE AN ILLUSION CREATED BY MY TORMENTED MIND TO PUNISH ME FOR THE FOUL THINGS I'VE DONE IN MY QUEST FOR THE MAGUS...
THEN AGAIN, I MAY NOT TRULY BE HERE!
... BUT THIS IS NOT THE TIME OR PLACE FOR SOUL-SEARCHING OR DOUBTS ABOUT MY SANITY!
I FEEL THE ROCK BENEATH MY FEET AND MY MIND IS QUITE CLEAR! THIS IS NO ILLUSION!
THIS IS REALITY, BUT A REALITY UNLIKE ANY I'VE EVER ENCOUNTERED BEFORE!
I'M AFRAID THAT'S NOT ENTIRELY TRUE, OL' FAITHFUL ONE!
WHO?!
YOU'VE ALWAYS BEEN IN THIS ACTUALITY, ADAM, OL' BOY!
YOU'VE JUST NEVER SEEN IT IN QUITE THIS MANNER BEFORE!
THE NAME'S LENTEAN, HEAD CLOWN AROUND HERE!
WELCOME TO "THE LAND OF THE WAY IT IS!"

WHAT ARE YOU TALKING ABOUT? WHERE AM I?
NOW TAKE IT EASY, TRUE BELIEVER! I'LL EXPLAIN AS WE GO ALONG!

YOU SEE, YOU'VE BEEN TERRIBLY SICK, ADAM, BUT OUR DOCTORS HAVE MADE YOU WELL!
NOW YOU CAN SEE THINGS AS THEY REALLY ARE! NO MORE MISCONCEPTIONS.
YOU CAN BE HAPPY NOW!
JUST FOLLOW ME AND I'LL SHOW YOU THE WAY TO THAT ETERNAL CONTENTMENT!
OH REALLY...

WE'RE HAVING A BIT OF TROUBLE HERE! VISUAL AND AUDIO PROGRAMMING IS BEING DISTORTED!
BUT I'M SURE IT'LL WORK ITSELF RIGHT ONCE WE BEGIN INDOCTRINATION!

"BEGIN WITH THE PERSONAL APPEARANCE PROGRAMMING!"
WELL, ADAM OL' PAL, OUR FIRST STEP ON THE ROAD TO JOY IS THE "HOW TO LOOK HAPPY ISLAND"!
THIS IS WHERE YOU SHED THOSE DARK ASPECTS THAT SET YOU APART FROM YOUR FELLOW CLOWNS!
BAG O TRICKS

THIS IS JAN HATROOMI! HE'S HERE TO SEE THAT EVERYONE APPEARS SOCIALLY ACCEPTABLE!
DO YOUR STUFF, JAN!
OOOOH! I LIKE THOSE EYES...

SPLOOT!
...BUT EVERYTHING ELSE MUST GO!

BEAUTIFUL, JAN, A TRUE MASTERPIECE!

ISN'T THAT MUCH NICER? NOW YOU CAN GO ANYWHERE AND LOOK LIKE EVERYONE ELSE!
YOU'LL BE MUCH HAPPIER BEING PART OF SOCIETY! IT'S MUCH BETTER THAN BEING AN OUTSIDER, A CRIMINAL OR A MADMAN!
WHAT DO YOU THINK OF YOUR NEW FACE?
A MASTERPIECE...?

LENS, IT'S TRUE THAT MANY OF THE THINGS THAT MAKE ME WHAT I AM MAY DISTURB OTHERS AS WELL AS MYSELF...
...BUT I DON'T BELIEVE COVERING THEM WITH PAINT AND RUBBER BALLS WILL DISPEL THEM!
TO HIDE THAT WHICH IS TRULY THERE WOULD BE A LIE!
I COULD NOT BE HAPPY LIVING IN SUCH A MANNER!
SURE, ADAM, HAVE IT YOUR OWN WAY!
WE'LL NOT FORCE YOU TO DO ANYTHING! WE'RE NOT TYRANTS HERE!
IF YOU WANT TO MAKE THINGS HARD FOR YOURSELF, GO RIGHT AHEAD!
THIS ISN'T GOING WELL AT ALL! THE DISTORTION IS GETTING WORSE, AND HE'S REBELLING!

IT'S THE EQUIVALENT OF MIDNIGHT ON HOMEWORLD, BIRTHPLACE OF THE UNIVERSAL CHURCH OF TRUTH!
THE ROYAL GUARD AT THE HOLY PALACE CHANGES WATCH AT THIS TIME!

RHA'GOR, A BLACK KNIGHT, HAS JUST BEEN RELIEVED OF DUTY FOR THE EVENING, AND NOW TRUDGES OFF INTO THE NIGHT!

HIS DESTINATION IS HOME AND REST!

HIS DESTINY IS IRON-STRONG FINGERS GRIPPING HIS TUNIC AND...

...COLD STEEL PRESSING AGAINST HIS THROAT!
I WISH TO SPEAK TO YOU!

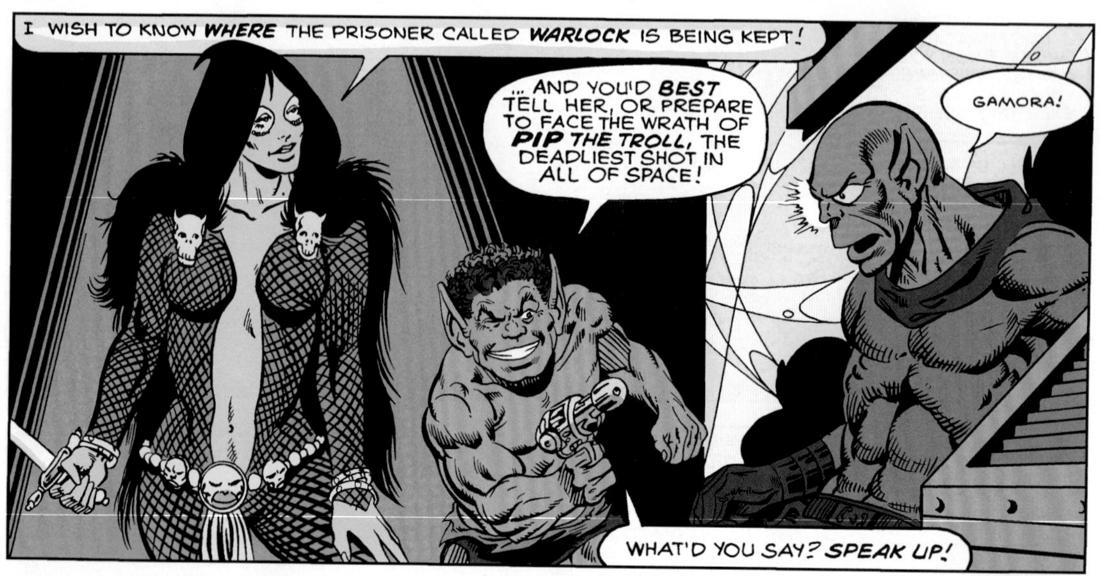
I WISH TO KNOW WHERE THE PRISONER CALLED WARLOCK IS BEING KEPT!
... AND YOU'D BEST TELL HER, OR PREPARE TO FACE THE WRATH OF PIP THE TROLL, THE DEADLIEST SHOT IN ALL OF SPACE!
GAMORA!
WHAT'D YOU SAY? SPEAK UP!

SURE... SURE, I'LL TELL YOU ANYTHING YOU WANT TO KNOW... JUST KEEP HER AWAY FROM ME!
HER?? LISTEN, I'M THE ONE YOU SHOULD BE SCARED OF...
OOPS!

HE'S BEING KEPT IN THF SUB-BASEMENT OF THE PALACE, THE SECTION CALLED THE PIT!
WHY THERE?
@#*$ GUN!

THAT'S WHERE THEY RECONDITION PEOPLE!
YOU'VE BEEN VERY HELPFUL! THANK YOU!
YOU MAY GO NOW!

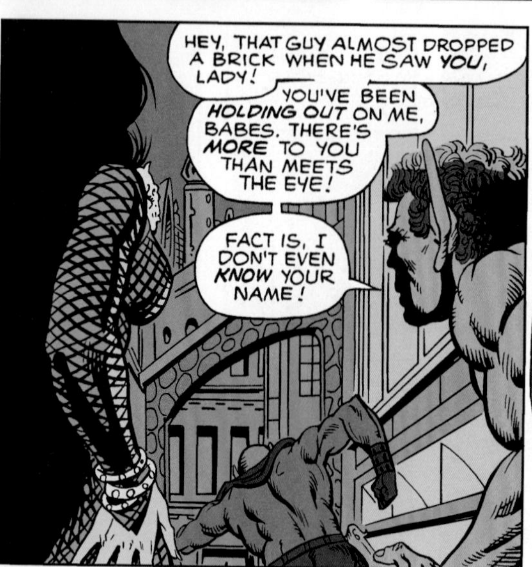
HEY, THAT GUY ALMOST DROPPED A BRICK WHEN HE SAW YOU, LADY!
YOU'VE BEEN HOLDING OUT ON ME, BABES. THERE'S MORE TO YOU THAN MEETS THE EYE!
FACT IS, I DON'T EVEN KNOW YOUR NAME!

I GO BY MANY NAMES, MY TICK-RIDDEN TROLL, BUT I'M SURE THE ONE THAT BLACK KNIGHT KNEW ME BY IS...
...GAMORA, THE DEADLIEST WOMAN IN THE WHOLE GALAXY!

MEANWHILE, BACK AT FANTASYLAND...!
WHAT'S THIS?
THIS IS SOMETHING I THOUGHT YOU SHOULD SEE!
THAT IS A RENEGADE CLOWN ON THE CROSS DOWN THERE!
IT'S A PITY. HE USED TO BE ONE OF THE BEST, BUT HE TRIED TO BUCK THE SYSTEM!
HE BEGAN TO THINK PEOPLE WERE MORE IMPORTANT THAN THINGS! HE EVEN BEGAN TO QUESTION "THE WAY THINGS ARE"!
SAD, ISN'T IT?

I TRIED! I PLAYED THE GAME AS LONG AS I COULD... JUST COULDN'T TAKE IT ANY LONGER... BUT YOU WOULDN'T UNDERSTAND!
THEN AGAIN, MAYBE I WOULD!

NOW ADAM, DON'T MISINTERPRET ALL THIS! WHAT WE'RE DOING HERE IS FOR THE CLOWN'S OWN GOOD AND FOR THE GOOD OF THE SYSTEM!
HEY!
WHAT ARE YOU GOING TO DO?

SPLOOT!

THIS IS OUTRAGEOUS! HIS PROGRAMMING HAS GONE COMPLETELY BERSERK!
HE'S JUST KNOCKED MY TWO ASSISTANTS UNCONSCIOUS!

THEN YOU'D BEST SUMMON NEW PROGRAMMERS AND FINISH THE TASK I'VE ASSIGNED YOU!
YOUR HOLINESS... THE MATRIARCH!!
I DIDN'T HEAR YOU ENTER!

THROUGH THE USE OF WILL-NUMBING ***DRUGS*** AND THE ***SENSORY INPUT HELMET*** WARLOCK IS WEARING, WE'RE ABLE TO IMPOSE SELECT SCENES UPON HIS CONSCIOUSNESS, DESIGNED TO ***CONVERT*** HIM OVER TO THE UNIVERSAL CHURCH'S WAY OF THINKING!

"IF WE'RE SUCCESSFUL, ***ADAM WARLOCK*** WILL BECOME OUR RELIGION'S GREATEST ***ZEALOT!***

"HE WOULD TAKE ***ANYTHING*** YOU SAY AS THE CHURCH'S HEAD AS ***ABSOLUTE TRUTH!*** HE'D BE YOUR ETERNAL ***SLAVE!***

"UNFORTUNATELY, WE'RE NOT DOING THAT ***WELL*** AT SUCCEEDING!

EXPLAIN THE GALAXY-SPANNING ***PROJECTS*** THE CHURCH IS WORKING ON! SHOW HIM THE ***GOOD*** HE CAN DO BY ***JOINING*** US!

PORTRAY THE CHURCH AS THE POOR STRUGGLING ***UNDERDOG*** AGAINST THE COSMIC GIANT ***ANARCHY!*** SUCCEED IN ***THIS*** AND HE IS ***OURS!***

I'LL CHECK BACK WITH YOU ***LATER!***

I'LL BE EXPECTING TO SEE ***RESULTS*** BY THEN!

WELL, THAT SHOULD ASSURE SUCCESS! WITH THE THREAT OF MY DISPLEASURE HANGING OVER HIS HEAD, PROF. TEANS WILL SHATTER ADAM'S 'OVERLY STRONG FREE WILL' IN RECORD TIME!
BEFORE THE DAY BREAKS, THAT GOLDEN GLADIATOR WILL BE MY EVER-OBEDIANT SERVANT!
STILL, IN A CERTAIN WAY, I'LL BE SAD TO SEE THAT HAPPEN!
CLOWNS... WHAT A MIND!

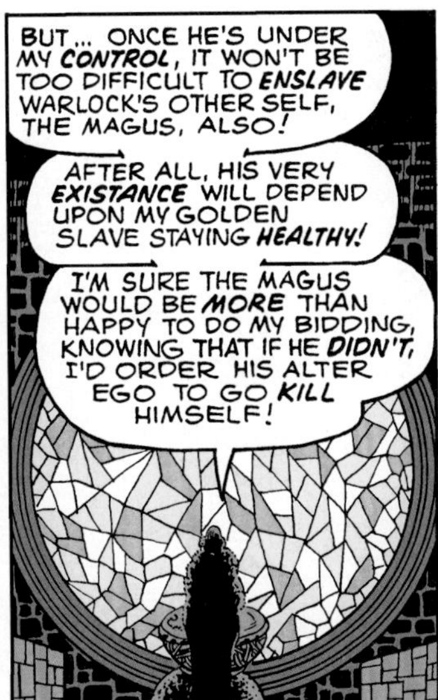
BUT... ONCE HE'S UNDER MY CONTROL, IT WON'T BE TOO DIFFICULT TO ENSLAVE WARLOCK'S OTHER SELF, THE MAGUS, ALSO!
AFTER ALL, HIS VERY EXISTANCE WILL DEPEND UPON MY GOLDEN SLAVE STAYING HEALTHY!
I'M SURE THE MAGUS WOULD BE MORE THAN HAPPY TO DO MY BIDDING, KNOWING THAT IF HE DIDN'T, I'D ORDER HIS ALTER EGO TO GO KILL HIMSELF!

I ONLY HOPE IT NEVER COMES TO THAT, FOR IF KILLING WARLOCK ELIMINATES ANY CHANCE OF THE MAGUS EXISTING... MY KINGDOM WILL NEVER COME INTO BEING, EITHER!
WELL, MY FINE LADY, IT'S ALL OR NOTHING THIS TIME! SO, ROLL THE DICE AND TO HELL WITH TOMORROW!
CLOWNS...

WHILE, LESS THAN A MILE AWAY...!
HEY!! WHERE WE GOING IN SUCH A HURRY?
TO FREE YOUR FRIEND WARLOCK!
BUT HE'S BEING HELD IN THE HOLY PALACE, AND THAT PLACE IS FULL OF HUNDREDS OF TRIGGER-HAPPY GUARDS!
YES, AND THEIR FAVORITE TARGETS ARE TROLLS!

STILL COMING?
SURE, RIGHT BEHIND YOU!

I MUST SAY, UP TO NOW YOU'VE NOT BEEN OVERLY COOPERATIVE, ADAM!
BUT I UNDER-STAND WHY!
YOU THINK WE'RE TRYING TO MOLD YOU INTO A DIFFERENT PERSON FOR OUR OWN PETTY PURPOSES RATHER THAN FOR YOUR OWN GOOD!
WELL, YOU'RE WRONG!

YOU SEE, WE'VE BEEN PREPARING YOU TO BECOME PART OF THIS... THE GREATEST WORK FORCE IN THE GALAXY!
WHAT ARE THOSE CLOWNS HAULING? WHY, IT LOOKS LIKE GARBAGE!

"WHY?!"

"WHY? BECAUSE THIS IS WHAT THEY'VE ALWAYS DONE AND ALWAYS WILL DO!"

"WAIT! LOOK! THE TOWER-- IT'S SWAYING! IT'S GOING TO COLLAPSE!

"ALL THOSE CLOWNS WILL BE KILLED!"

"RELAX, ADAM! THIS ALSO ALWAYS HAPPENS! WE'VE COME TO EXPECT IT!"

"WHY?

"WHY?

"WHY?"

BUT IT'S THE ONLY MADNESS WE HAVE!
WELL, YOU CAN KEEP IT! I WANT NOTHING TO DO WITH A WORLD POPULATED BY CLOWNS THAT WASTE THEIR LIVES BUILDING TOWERS OF RUBBISH!
IF ONLY I COULD BE SURE HOW TO LEAVE THIS STRANGE WORLD!

A NORMAL PLANET I'D SIMPLY LEVITATE OFF OF!
BUT THIS PLACE... I JUST CAN'T FIGURE OUT EXACTLY WHICH WAY IS UP OR DOWN, TO OR FROM!
WHAT'S THIS?

IT LOOKS LIKE THYAMITE, THE STRONGEST AND MOST BEAUTIFUL SUBSTANCE KNOWN OF THROUGHOUT THE GALAXY!
WHAT'S IT DOING IN THIS GARBAGE HEAP?

OH, THAT STUFF! WE JUST CAN'T SEEM TO KEEP IT OUT OF OUR REFUSE!
SOMEONE KEEPS PUTTING IT IN WHILE WE'RE NOT LOOKING!
I SUSPECT THAT'S WHY THE TOWER KEEPS COLLAPSING!

DIAMONDS AMONG THE GARBAGE!
LET ME OUT OF HERE!

THERE HAS TO BE AN ESCAPE ROUTE FROM THIS CRAZY WORLD!
THERE IS!
BUT IT'S TOO DANGEROUS!

I DON'T CARE ABOUT THE PERIL! I HAVE TO GET OFF THIS WORLD BEFORE I LOSE MY MIND!

BUT THAT IS THE ONLY WAY OUT!
THE ONLY EXIT IS THROUGH THE DOORWAY OF MADNESS!

REALITY!
THIS LOOKS LIKE IT'S AS FAR AS WE'RE GOING TO GET BY BEING SNEAKY, TOOTS!
I BELIEVE IT'S TIME TO GET VIOLENT!

FOR ONCE I AGREE WITH YOU!
LET'S TAKE THEM!

WAHOOO!
THIS IS MORE FUN THAN BROWN EYEING!
WELL, RESTRAIN THAT OVERLY ENTHUSIASTIC ATTITUDE, MAGGOT!
WE NEED ONE OF THESE TECHNOS CONSCIOUS TO HELP US FIND WARLOCK!
WITCH, THE ONLY THING YOU'LL FIND HERE IS...

...DEATH!
MY... HOW MELO-DRAMATIC!

UNFORTUNATELY, YOUR FLAIR FOR DYNAMIC ENTRANCES FAR SURPASSES ANY FIGHTING SKILL AN ICE BLUE CRETIN SUCH AS YOURSELF MIGHT POSSESS!

DON'T WORRY, BABES! I'LL HANDLE THIS CRUMB SNEAKING UP BEHIND YOU!
YOU MEATBAG! I WAS WELL PREPARED TO HANDLE HIS CLUMSY ATTACK!

I WANTED MERELY TO RESTRAIN THAT ONE, NOT TOTAL HIM!
NOW, BECAUSE YOU ENJOY BASHING HEADS, WE'RE GOING TO HAVE TO SEARCH THIS WHOLE LAB TO FIND WARLOCK!
SORRY, IT'S JUST THAT I ENJOY MY WORK AND TEND TO GET OVERLY ZEALOUS!
NIGHTMARE!
HOW MUCH FARTHER TO THIS DOOR? IT SEEMS WE'VE BEEN WALKING THROUGH THESE COSMIC CORRIDORS FOR HOURS!
JUST OVER HERE!
SORRY ABOUT THE DISTANCE!
BUT IF WE KEPT THIS DOOR OF MADNESS ANY CLOSER, IT MIGHT PROVE TOO MUCH OF A TEMPTATION FOR SOME OF THE WEAKER CLOWNS!
THERE IT IS!
AGAIN, I BEG YOU TO RECONSIDER!
ONCE YOU GO THROUGH THAT DOOR, YOU MAY NEVER BE ABLE TO RETURN!
YOU DON'T KNOW WHAT IT MAY BE LIKE IN THERE!
IT MIGHT BE A LIVING NIGHTMARE...
...OR A WELCOME REST!
WHATEVER AWAITS ME BEYOND THIS THRESHOLD... I WELCOME!
BETTER THE FREEDOM OF MADNESS THAN THE IMPRISONMENT OF THIS INSANE WORLD!
THOOM!
WELCOME TO THE REALM OF SCHIZOPHRENIA, PARANOIA, AND ANYTHING ELSE YOU MAY CARE TO EXPLORE!
WHO?!
WHO?

I AM RELEASE! I'M YOUR ESCAPE TO FANTASY!
I'M EVERYTHING YOU SEEK! I'M THE MADNESS MONSTER!

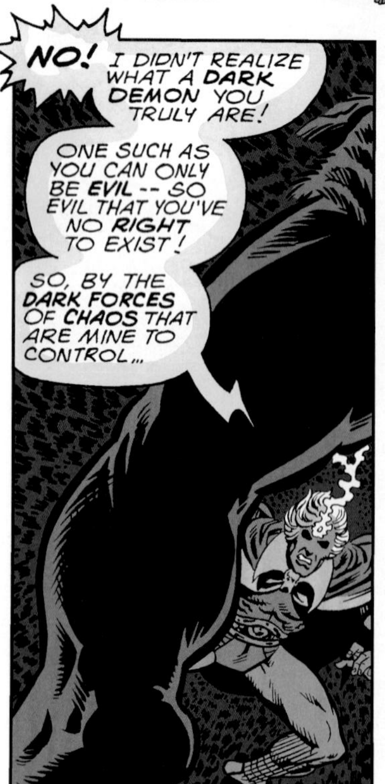

FOOL!
YOUR FOUL GEM CANNOT AFFECT ONE WHO HAS NO SOUL!
NO SOUL! HOW?!
ARGG!
I'VE NO NEED FOR A SOUL OF MY OWN!
I AM PART... YOU ARE WHOLE!
OF COURSE, YOU'RE PART OF MY SOUL!
YOU'RE THAT DARK SLICE OF MYSELF THAT I'VE ALWAYS KEPT BURIED AND FEAR ABOVE ALL ELSE!
YOU'RE THAT BLACK SECTION OF MY SOUL THAT...
...CREATED THE MAGUS!
ABSOLUTELY CORRECT!
I'M THE TWISTED EVIL THAT INFESTS YOUR INNER SELF!
I'M ALL THOSE FOUL THINGS YOU'VE NEVER DARED SAY OR DO!
I'M THE MADNESS MONSTER!

IT'S TRUE, YOU'VE ALWAYS BEEN WITH ME, YET I'VE DENIED YOU!

THE GOSSAMER VEIL OF FALSE MORALITY HAS BEEN LIFTED FROM MY EYES! I NOW SEE YOU CLEARLY!

YOU'RE NEITHER DEMON NOR ANGEL! YOU'RE MERELY A DIFFERENT POINT OF VIEW... NO MORE THAN A DIFFERENT...

...REALITY!

WELCOME BACK TO IT! WE WERE ABOUT TO UNPLUG YOU, BUT IT APPEARS YOU'VE SAVED US THE TROUBLE!

INCREDIBLE! HE'S SHORTED OUT THE INPUT HELMET BY PURE FORCE OF WILL ALONE!

NO ONE'S EVER DONE THAT BEFORE!

THAT'S PROBABLY BECAUSE NONE OF YOUR PREVIOUS PATIENTS EVER DARED ENTER YOUR DOORWAY TO MADNESS BEFORE!
SUCH A TERRIFYING YET INVALUABLE EXPERIENCE GAINS FOR A PERSON AN INCREDIBLE PERCEPTION OF ONE'S OWN INNER WORKINGS!
FOR THE FIRST TIME I UNDERSTAND THE MAGUS!

BUT I'VE HAD TO PAY A HIGH PRICE FOR THIS KNOWLEDGE!
YOU SEE, I HAD TO SURRENDER MYSELF TO MADNESS! WHAT I MEAN IS, WELL, I'M NOW QUITE INSANE!

I NOW SEE THINGS AS THE MAGUS DOES, YET I'VE NOT ABANDONED MY OTHER VIEWS OF REALITY AS HE'S DONE!
THIS ALTERATION IN THOUGHT MAY NOW GIVE ME THE INSIGHT NECESSARY TO DEFEAT THE MAGUS! OR...
...IT MAY DESTROY ME!

THEN AGAIN, IT MAY GIVE ME THE FINAL VICTORY I SEEK!
YOU!
I SENSED YOU WERE NEAR!

I SEE... YOUR ALTERED CONSCIOUSNESS IS BEGINNING TO WORK FOR YOU ALREADY!
YOU SEEM SURPRISED THAT I'M AWARE OF THE CHANGE WITHIN YOU!

YOU STILL REFUSE TO ACCEPT ME AS YOUR FUTURE -- JUST AS I REMEMBER!

DO YOU ALSO 'RECALL' THAT THIS IS THE MOMENT THAT I FINALLY REALIZED THAT YOU ARE NOT ALL YOU PRETEND TO BE!

OF COURSE, YOU'VE FINALLY PENETRATED MY DISGUISE!

MY 'WIZARD OF OZ' DECEPTION HAS SERVED ITS PURPOSE!
SO AT LAST I CAN FINALLY REVEAL MY TRUE SELF TO YOU!

I AM THE TRUE MAGUS!
MY PLANS REQUIRED A STAND-IN UP TILL NOW! I NEEDED TO KEEP YOU OFF-BALANCE... UNCERTAIN!
OTHERWISE, YOU MIGHT HAVE BEEN ABLE TO ALTER MY PAST-- YOUR FUTURE!
BUT THE DANGER OF THAT HAPPENING HAS PASSED! WE'VE COME TOO FAR DOWN THE PATH OF MY CREATION!
YOU'VE LOST, WARLOCK!
THERE IS ABSOLUTELY NOTHING YOU CAN DO TO CHANGE WHAT'S ABOUT TO OCCUR!
NEXT: MADNESS IN THE HOUSE OF THE MAGUS!

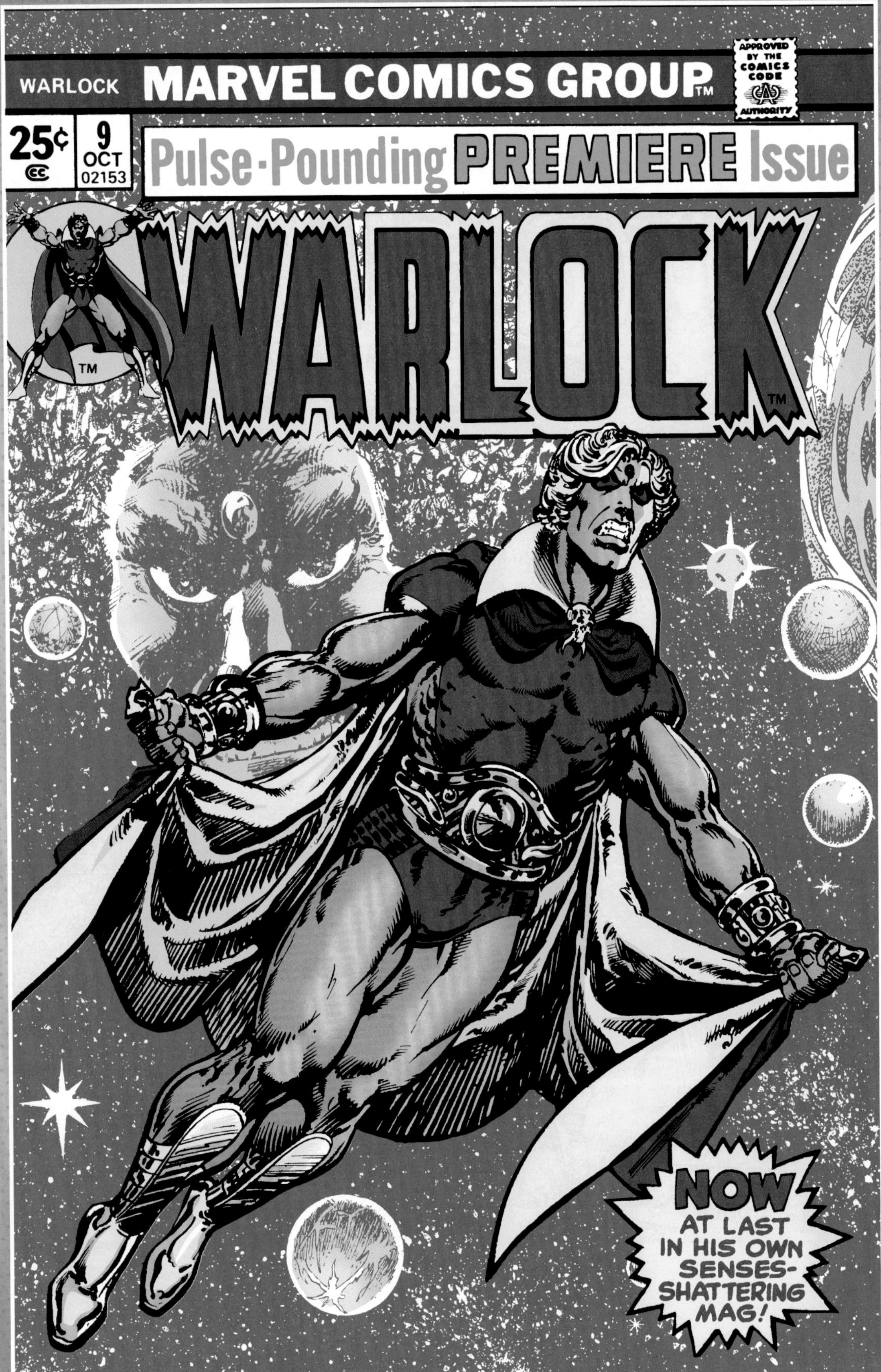

WARLOCK MARVEL COMICS GROUP™

25¢ 9 OCT 02153

Pulse-Pounding PREMIERE Issue

WARLOCK™

NOW AT LAST IN HIS OWN SENSES-SHATTERING MAG!

Born to be Earth's man of the future, then forced to abandon his native planet because of his alien ways, he wanders the stars seeking **LIFE!** Gifted with ultra-strength, paranormal reflexes and perceptions, the power of levitation and the curse of a vampire soul-gem, he stands uniquely **ALONE** among the heavens.

STAN LEE PRESENTS: THE POWER OF WARLOCK!™

FUSSING LEN WEIN * BLOTTING STEVE LEIALOHA * SCRIBBLING TOM ORZECHOWSKI * EVERYTHING ELSING JIM STARLIN

AND SO...
HOLY GOOSH! THAT'S THE MAGUS!?
HE LOOKS JUST LIKE YOU, ADAM, 'CEPT HE'S SILVER AND HAS AN ELECTRO HAIR-DO!
FLEA BAG, THE DIFFERENCE IS FAR MORE PRONOUNCED THAN THAT, I ASSURE YOU!
I AM THE BUTTERFLY THIS GOLDEN CATERPILLAR BEFORE YOU SHALL SOON METAMORPHOSE INTO!

I AM THE NEW ORDER!
I AM THAT WHICH THE FORCES OF CHAOS AND ORDER HAVE DECREED YOU SHALL BECOME!
MAGUS... YOU'RE NOTHING... BUT A COLD-BLOODED TYRANT...
...WHO THINKS HIMSELF GOD!

YOU'VE CAUSED UNBEARABLE SUFFERING AND GRIEF TO THE THOUSAND WORLDS..., TO THE BILLIONS OF PEOPLE YOU'VE ENSLAVED!
YOU'RE AN INTOLERABLE CANCER IN THE VERY HEART OF THE UNIVERSE AND MUST BE STOPPED FROM INFECTING THE REMAINDER OF THE STARS!
AND WHO, PRAY TELL, IS TO STOP ME?

HA HA HA HA HA HA HA HA
ME!

YOU POOR FOOL! YOUR EGO BETRAYS YOU!
YOU STILL BELIEVE YOU CAN STRUGGLE AGAINST THE UNJUST WHIMS OF FATE AND CREATE YOUR OWN DESTINY!
YOU REFUSE TO BELIEVE YOU'RE NOTHING MORE OR LESS THAN WHAT THE POWERS OF CHAOS AND ORDER WISH YOU TO BE!

THOSE POWERS HAVE SELECTED YOU TO WEAR THE MANTLE OF GODHOOD!
YOU'VE NO CHOICE BUT TO ACCEPT!

YOU ARE DESTINED TO BECOME THAT WHICH IS ME!
FOR EVERYTHING THAT NOW TRANSPIRES I'VE EXPERIENCED BEFORE...
...AS YOU!

NO!
I REFUSE TO BELIEVE I'M TO BECOME AS EVIL AS YOU!

YOU'VE FORCED MILLIONS INTO SLAVERY, WHILE FREEDOM IS MY LIFE'S BLOOD!
YOU LIVE BY TERROR, VIOLENCE AND DECEIT, WHILE TRUTH AND PEACE ARE MY ONLY LIGHTS!
YOU ARE EVERYTHING I OPPOSE, YET YOU CLAIM WE ARE ONE!

HOW?! HOW CAN SUCH AS THIS BE?
WAIT!! WHAT ARE YOU DOING?

MERELY REPEATING WORDS I ONCE SPOKE IN IGNORANCE!
AS FOR "HOW"... MIGHT I NOT BE THE OTHER SIDE OF THE COIN THAT IS YOU!
I SEE THAT ANSWER IS NOT QUITE SATIS-FACTORY, IS IT?

THEN HOW DOES THIS SUIT YOU!
DO YOU RECALL OUR FIRST MEETING? I HAD...
...JUST HAD A YOUNG GIRL MURDERED!

I USED HER AS BAIT! I KNEW HER DEATH WOULD SEND YOU AFTER ME SEEKING VENGEANCE!
EVENTUALLY, YOUR SEARCH CONFRONTED YOU WITH THE MATRIARCH, THE TEMPORAL LEADER OF MY UNIVERSAL CHURCH OF TRUTH!

THE MATRIARCH, UNSATISFIED WITH THE POWERS I GRANTED HER, HOPED THAT, THROUGH YOU, SHE MIGHT OVERTHROW MY RULE, AND HERSELF BECOME OMNIPOTENT HEAD OF MY HOLY EMPIRE!

SHE SOON REALIZED THAT KILLING YOU MIGHT CAUSE THE RELIGIOUS DOMAIN SHE RULED OVER TO CEASE TO EXIST!

SO SHE RESORTED TO ELECTRONIC BRAINWASHING, HOPING THAT ENSLAVING YOU WOULD DO THE SAME TO ME!

ALL THIS OCCURRED JUST AS I RECALLED IT HAD, SO I CONTENTED MYSELF WITH MERE OBSERVATION UNTIL...

...IN ORDER TO BE FREE OF THE MATRIARCH'S MENTAL DESPOTISM YOUR MIND ESCAPED INTO MADNESS...

...JUST AS I HAD PLANNED IT TO DO!
FOR, YOU SEE...
...IT'S IMPORTANT THAT YOU BECOME ADJUSTED TO MY DISTORTED THOUGHT PROCESSES AND ALTERED PERCEPTIONS IN STAGES...

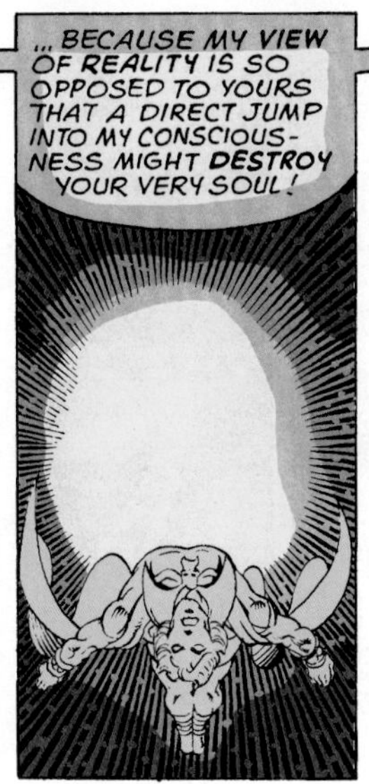
...BECAUSE MY VIEW OF REALITY IS SO OPPOSED TO YOURS THAT A DIRECT JUMP INTO MY CONSCIOUSNESS MIGHT DESTROY YOUR VERY SOUL!

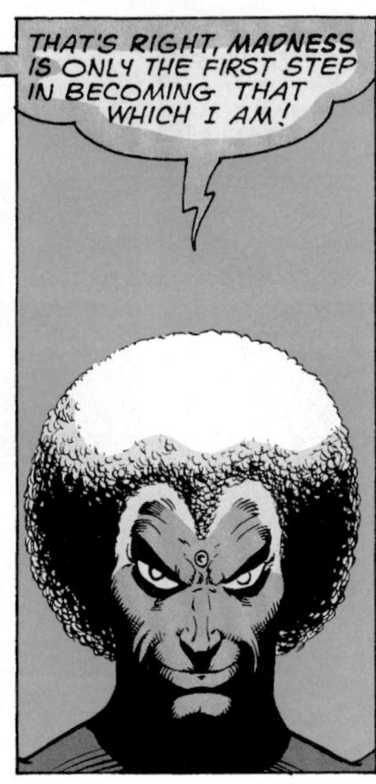
THAT'S RIGHT, MADNESS IS ONLY THE FIRST STEP IN BECOMING THAT WHICH I AM!

YOUR TRANSFORMATION WILL NOT BE COMPLETE UNTIL THE HIDDEN POWERS WHISPER THEIR DARK "SECRETS" TO YOU!
HEY, LADY-- CAN'T YOU SEE? ADAM'S IN TROUBLE!
DO SOMETHING!

I'M AFRAID I CAN'T JUST YET!
BUT I BELIEVE IT'S TIME YOU "BECAME INVOLVED"!
WELL, SOME "MOST DANGEROUS WOMAN IN THE GALAXY" YOU TURNED OUT TO BE!
OKAY! IF THAT'S THE WAY IT'S GOING TO BE...

...LOOK OUT WORLD, 'CAUSE HERE COMES PIP THE GOD-BASHER!

YOU KNOW, I'VE WAITED OVER 5,000 YEARS TO DO THIS!

NOW THAT WE'RE ALONE, I CAN FINISH RELATING MY ORIGIN TO YOU!
FOR, WHAT I'M ABOUT TO TELL YOU IS BEST RESERVED FOR OUR EARS ALONE!

I STAND MERE STEPS FROM THE MAGUS, YET HE REMAINS UNAWARE OF MY PRESENCE!
WHAT DO YOU INSTRUCT?

WAIT!
WAIT UNTIL THE MOMENT WE'VE AGREED UPON, FOR THE MAGUS' GODLIKE SENSES...
...MAY YET BREACH THAT DEFENSE HIS OWN NATURE HAS GIVEN US!

BUT WHEN THAT POINT IN TIME ARRIVES, STRIKE WITH EVERY OUNCE OF SPEED AND STRENGTH I'VE GIVEN YOU!
THE VERY FATE OF THE STARS RESTS WITH YOU!
YES, MASTER!

"WHO IS THE MYSTERIOUS 'MASTER,'" YOU ASK? "WHAT ARE THESE 'DARK SECRETS' THE MAGUS SPEAKS OF... AND WHAT THE DEVIL IS GAMORA UP TO?"
WELL, JUST HANG IN THERE, READER, BECAUSE EVERYTHING IS ABOUT TO BE EXPLAINED AWAY, TO EVERYONE'S SATISFACTION! -- LEN.
I HOPE! -- JIM.
MEANWHILE, BACK TO OUR TRIUMPHANT ARCH-FIEND!

WELL, MY GOLD-SKINNED ALTER EGO, UP TO NOW I'VE SIMPLY EXPLAINED THOSE THINGS THAT HAVE ALREADY HAPPENED TO YOU!
WE'VE REACHED THE POINT WHERE YOU MUST NOW HEAR OF WHAT'S PLANNED FOR YOUR FUTURE!

BY THE TIME I FINISH MY LITTLE TALE, YOU'LL HAVE REGAINED THE STRENGTH MY JEWEL'S RAY-BURST HAS SAPPED FROM YOU AND...
...YOU'LL ATTACK ME! AND ONCE AGAIN I'LL BLAST YOU WITH MY SOUL GEM!
ONLY THIS TIME THE RAY'S EFFECT WILL BE QUITE DIFFERENT!

"THE BEAM WILL SATURATE YOUR BODY WITH A HARMLESS RADIATION WHICH SHALL ACT AS A BEACON TO GUIDE HE, WHOM I WISH TO SUMMON!

"THE HEAVENS WILL OPEN AND HE WILL STEP FORTH!
"A DREAM WILL PASS AND HE WILL BE BEFORE YOU!
"YOU'LL SUDDENLY REALIZE IT'S DAWN AND HE WILL TOUCH YOU!

"HE IS KNOWN AS THE IN-BETWEENER!
"HIS REALM; THAT SPACE BETWEEN FACT AND FANTASY!
"YOU WILL STRIVE TO ELUDE HIM, BUT THE RADIATION EMANATING FROM YOUR BODY WILL UNFAILINGLY LEAD HIM TO YOU!

"SO, EXACTLY THREE HOURS AFTER HE HAS BEEN CALLED, THE IN-BETWEENER SHALL REACH OUT AND...

"...TOUCH YOU, THUS TRANSPORTING YOU INSTANTLY TO HIS OWN BIZARRE DOMAIN!
"THERE YOU WILL LEARN THAT HIS IS THE LAND BETWEEN REALITY AND ILLUSION... TIME AND SPACE!

"THERE, YOU WILL FLOAT FOR COUNTLESS CENTURIES, UNABLE TO DO NAUGHT SAVE EXIST!
"THERE WE SHALL LEARN THOSE 'DARK SECRETS' THE POWERS OF CHAOS AND ORDER WISH TO WHISPER TO US!
"IT WAS THERE WE LEARNED THAT QUALITIES SUCH AS GOOD AND EVIL ARE NOTHING MORE THAN LIES CREATED BY MAN TO CONTROL MAN!
"IT WAS THERE I LEARNED THE GREAT DIVISION IS NOT RIGHT OR WRONG, BUT... PURPOSE OR DEATH!

"I SOUGHT REFUGE FROM THESE 'TRUTHS' WITHIN MY PROTECTIVE COCOON, BUT THEY FOLLOWED AND ATE AWAY AT MY EVERY THOUGHT, IMPULSE, AND VALUE!

"FINALLY THE WHISPERS BECAME THE ONLY TRUTH! MY PAST, AT LAST, WAS REVEALED AS A LIE, AND MY ONLY REALITY TURNED INTO TOTAL MADNESS!

THUS ENLIGHTENED, I RETURNED TO THIS ACTUALITY AND BURST FREE FROM MY COCOON, AT LAST TRULY THE MAGUS!

"THE PEOPLE WERE, EVEN THEN, SCIENTIFICALLY ADVANCED, YET THEY REMAINED A SUPERSTITIOUS LOT!

"UPON MAKING CONTACT, THEY IMMEDIATELY ATTACKED, THINKING ME A DEMON OF SOME TYPE!

"SO, I SHOWED THEM HOW A DEMON PROTECTS HIMSELF!

"FORTUNATELY, THE YEARS OF INCUBATION WITHIN MY CHRYSALIS HAD GIVEN ME THOSE POWERS THAT YOU HAD FORSAKEN WHEN YOU LEFT THE COCOON TO AID THE HIGH EVOLUTIONARY! *

*SEE MARVEL PREMIERE #1. --LEN.

"I THEN SET ABOUT FORMING THE UNIVERSAL CHURCH OF TRUTH! I MEAN, WHAT GOOD IS A GOD WITHOUT A CHURCH?
"LIKE MOST RELIGIONS, IT WAS CREATED TO KEEP ITS PRACTITIONERS IN LINE BY THREATS OF DAMNATION AND SUCH!

"YET, MY CHURCH WOULD BE WEDDED TO THE PLANET'S GOVERNMENT THUS INSTILLING A RELIGIOUS STAMP OF APPROVAL ON ANY TASK I FELT THE PLANET SHOULD UNDERTAKE FOR ME!
"THE FIRST SUCH PROJECT WAS A HOLY WAR UPON THE HEATHENS THAT INFESTED OUR NEIGHBORING PLANETS!

"IT WAS GREAT... EVERY COUPLE OF YEARS, MY GRAND INQUISITORS, WHO PREACHED PEACE AND LOVE, WOULD DEVASTATE A WORLD WHICH, IN MOST CASES, WAS PRACTICING PEACE AND LOVE!
"THAT WAS THE WAY THE WORD OF THE MAGUS SPREAD!

"OVER A THOUSAND WORLDS ARE NOW MINE TO COMMAND! TO COUNTLESS BILLIONS OF SOULS I AM GOD, RIGHT OR WRONG!
"--AS I'LL SOMEDAY BE TO ALL LIVING CREATURES THROUGH-OUT THE STARS!

"BUT ONLY IF I EXISTED! FOUR YEARS AGO I BEGAN TO PLAN IN EARNEST FOR THIS VERY NIGHT!
"I HAD CENTURIES BEFORE I ADOPTED MY 'WIZARD OF OZ' DISGUISE FOR ITS SHOCK VALUE, AND ESTABLISHED THE BLACK KNIGHTS, PALACE INQUISITORS, AND ANY OTHER GROUP I REMEMBERED YOU MEETING!
"ALL THAT REALLY NEEDED TO BE DONE WAS TO FIND AND RELINQUISH PHYSICAL CONTROL OF THE CHURCH TO THE MATRIARCH!

"AT LAST, I LOCATED HER IN A CERTAIN SINFUL ESTABLISHMENT IN ONE OF THIS VERY CITY'S LOWEST LEVELS!
"THERE SHE WAS KNOWN AS AN INFAMOUS WOMAN OF EASY MORALS, WITH AN IRON WILL AND A MIND LIKE A RAZOR!
"SHE WAS MAGNIFICENT! SHE TOOK CONTROL OF MY HOLY EMPIRE AS IF SHE WERE BORN TO DO SO, AS WELL SHE MAY HAVE BEEN!

"A PITY IT WAS PREORDAINED THAT SHE BETRAY ME!
"UNFORTUNATELY, EVERY GOD NEEDS HIS JUDAS!

"AT LAST THE STAGE WAS SET! ALL I HAD TO DO FROM THAT POINT WAS SIT BACK AND WATCH ALL THAT HAD HAPPENED TO ME, IN CENTURIES PAST, NOW HAPPENING TO YOU!"
"THEN TELL ME, MAGUS..."

...DID I DO THIS LAST TIME AROUND?

YES, AND THIS IS EXACTLY THE WAY I REACTED TO YOUR EFFORTS!

NOW THINGS SHOULD REALLY BEGIN TO HAPPEN!
YOU'LL NOW GET UP AND RESUME YOUR FUTILE ATTACK AND...

...I'LL RESPOND LIKE SO!
NO!

THOUGHT THAT WAS THE RADIATION BURST THAT WOULD SIGNAL THE IN-BETWEENER, DIDN'T YOU?
NO, WE'VE A FEW MINUTES BEFORE THAT'S DUE!
SO I THOUGHT WE'D KILL SOME TIME PLAYING AN OLD EARTH GAME I REMEMBER CALLED TAG!
GUESS WHAT... YOU'RE IT!

THE OBJECT OF THIS GAME IS TO CATCH ME IF YOU CAN!
HAHA HA HA HA HA HA HA HA
THEN CATCH YOU I SHALL, AND WHEN I DO, YOU'LL PAY FOR THE EVIL YOU'VE CAUSED!

BY THE STARS, HOW YOU'LL PAY!

TELL ME, DOES THAT USUALLY SEND SHIVERS DOWN THE BACKS OF YOUR ADVERSARIES?
YOU SHOULD TRY THIS SOMETIME AND WATCH THEIR REACTIONS!
WHAT?!

BUT YOU DON'T SEEM ABLE TO DO THAT, DO YOU?
THEN I'LL JUST HAVE TO COME OUT, WON'T I?
WE'VE GOT TO PLAY FAIR NOW, DON'T WE?

... AND AS OUR GOLDEN GLADIATOR STRUGGLES ON...
LOOK OUT!
ONE TROLL COMING THROUGH!

LISTEN, GAMORA! I DON'T KNOW WHAT YOU'RE WAITING FOR, BUT ADAM NEEDS YOUR HELP REALLY BAD!
I'D HELP HIM MYSELF BUT...

YOU SEE... I'M GOING... TO BE BUSY... FOR... ULP... THE NEXT... GAG... FEW MINUTES... OOOOOH!
MY TIME HAS NOT YET COME! SOON, PIP, SOON!
RIGHT, MASTER?

CORRECT, GAMORA!
THE MAGUS IS SO SURE THAT ALL WILL HAPPEN AS BEFORE THAT HIS SENSES...
...REFUSE TO ACCEPT THE FACT THAT YOU, A FOREIGN ELEMENT, HAVE ENTERED HIS REALITY!

YET WAIT UNTIL HE IS COMPLETELY ENGROSSED WITH SUMMONING THE IN-BETWEENER BEFORE YOU STRIKE...
... WITH THAT SPECIALLY TEMPERED DAGGER, WHOSE BLADE WILL EVEN SLAY ONE SUCH AS THE MAGUS!

I'VE TRAINED YOU SO THAT THE MAGUS' DISTORTION WILL NOT HINDER YOU!
NOW! THE MOMENT IS UPON US! YOU NEED WAIT...

...NO LONGER! IT'S TIME THIS DARK COMEDY CAME TO AN END!
I'LL ALLOW YOU ONE LAST LOOK ABOUT YOU, WARLOCK, FOR YOUR LIFE IS ABOUT TO END AS MINE IS ABOUT TO TRULY BEGIN!

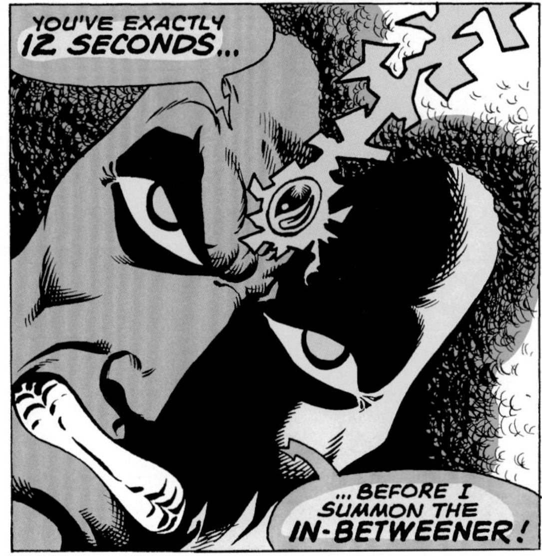
YOU'VE EXACTLY 12 SECONDS...
...BEFORE I SUMMON THE IN-BETWEENER!

12

11 11

10 10

9 9

8 8

7 7

6 6

5 5 5

4 4 4

3 3

2 2 2
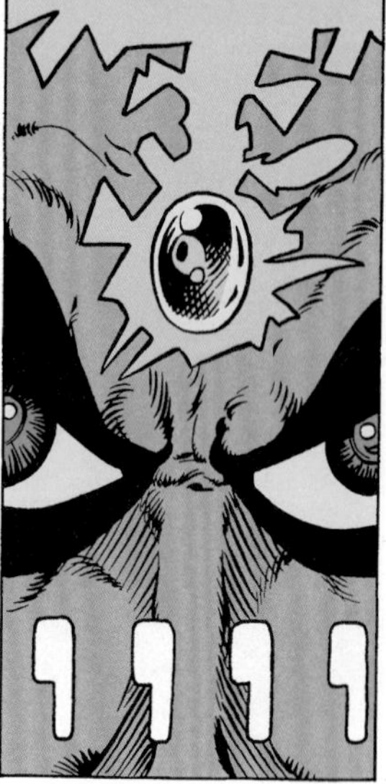
1 1 1 1

...ZERO

AN **EMERALD RAY** LASHES OUT, AND EVEN THOUGH IT CAUSES NO PAIN, A BLOOD-CURDLING SCREAM OF ANGUISH SPRINGS FROM THE **SOUL** OF **ADAM WARLOCK!**

NYEEEARGH!

FOR HE KNOWS THAT **NOTHING** WILL EVER BE AS LIGHT, CAREFREE, OR HAPPY AS THOSE DAYS PAST, NOW **LOST** FOREVER!

DON'T WORRY, ADAM! MY MASTER WILL THINK OF...
WORRY! WHY SHOULD I WORRY? I'M ABOUT TO BECOME A GOD!
I'VE BEEN A GOD BEFORE, YOU KNOW!

BACK ON COUNTER-EARTH, THEY THOUGHT OF ME AS THEIR MESSIAH!
I WAS SENT TO DELIVER THEM FROM EVIL!

BY ORION! IF ONLY THEY COULD SEE ME NOW!
I WAS THE GODLING THAT SAVED THEM FROM THE SINISTER SCHEMES OF THE MAN-BEAST AND GAVE THEM THE GIFT OF PEACE...
...AND NOW I CAN'T EVEN SAVE MYSELF FROM MYSELF!
BY THE STARS, LOOK WHAT I'VE BECOME!

I NOW STAND BEFORE YOU... A STEALER OF SOULS!
FIRST, THERE WAS AUTOLYCUS. TRUE, MY SOUL GEM ACTED ON ITS OWN THAT TIME...
...BUT I ORDERED IT TO TEAR THE LIFE FORCE FROM KRA-TOR, THE GRAND INQUISITOR!
*SEE STRANGE TALES #179-180.

THAT MAKES ME WORSE THAN ANY MURDERER, MY FRIENDS!
I'VE BECOME A SPIRITUAL VAMPIRE!
FROM SAVIOR TO VAMPIRE, AND SOON TO BE MAD MONARCH OF A THOUSAND WORLDS... THAT'S ME!

NO... I'VE ABSOLUTELY NOTHING TO WORRY ABOUT... I'M ABOUT TO BECOME EVERYTHING A PERSON COULD WISH FOR!
PEOPLE WILL WORSHIP ME! I'LL HAVE THE POWER TO DO ANYTHING I WANT AND...

...ALL IT'S GOING TO COST ME IS... MY HUMANITY!

MEANWHILE, ELSEWHERE IN THE HOLY PALACE...

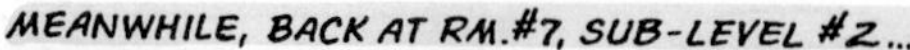
MEANWHILE, BACK AT RM.#7, SUB-LEVEL #2...

I HATE TO BE THE ONE THAT HAS TO SAY THIS, BUT...
...IT LOOKS TO ME LIKE THE UNIVERSE'S GREAT GOLDEN HOPE HAS DONE GONE TO PIECES!

I'D BEST INFORM THE MASTER OF OUR SITUATION!
THERE IS NO NEED TO, GAMORA!
I'VE BEEN OBSERVING THE PROCEEDINGS WITH THE UTMOST INTEREST!

I'VE ALSO DETERMINED THE BEST COURSE OF ACTION FOR US TO FOLLOW!
STAND BACK! I'M ABOUT TO PHASE INTO YOUR SPHERE OF EXISTENCE TO TAKE PERSONAL CONTROL OF THE SITUATION!

I MUST ADMIT THAT I SEVERELY UNDER-ESTIMATED THE MAGUS' POWER!

I HAD HOPED GAMORA'S INTERFERENCE INTO THE MAGUS' PAST-PRESENT REALITY MIGHT BE POWERFUL ENOUGH TO DISRUPT THAT WHICH HAS BEEN AND WILL BE!

SO, I MUST NOW IMPOSE A NEW ELEMENT INTO THE MAGUS' FANTASY-REALITY THAT HE WON'T BE ABLE TO DISMISS WITH THE BACK OF HIS HAND...

...AND I ASSURE YOU **THANOS** IS SUCH AN ELEMENT!

I HAD HOPED TO AVOID **PERSONAL INVOLVEMENT** IN THIS AFFAIR, FOR OTHER, MORE **IMPORTANT** MATTERS NOW SCREAM FOR MY ATTENTION!

YET, THOSE PLANS **DEPEND** ON WARLOCK'S CONTINUED WELL-BEING, SO I FIND THAT I AM FORCED TO **INTERVENE!**

SO THANOS NOW STANDS **WITH** YOU, ADAM WARLOCK, PREPARED TO **FIGHT** TO THE **DEATH!**

NEXT:
WARLOCK
AND
THANOS
BATTLE SIDE BY SIDE AGAINST A
WORLD!!

WARLOCK MARVEL COMICS GROUP™

APPROVED BY THE COMICS CODE AUTHORITY

25¢ CC

10 DEC 02153

WARLOCK™

™

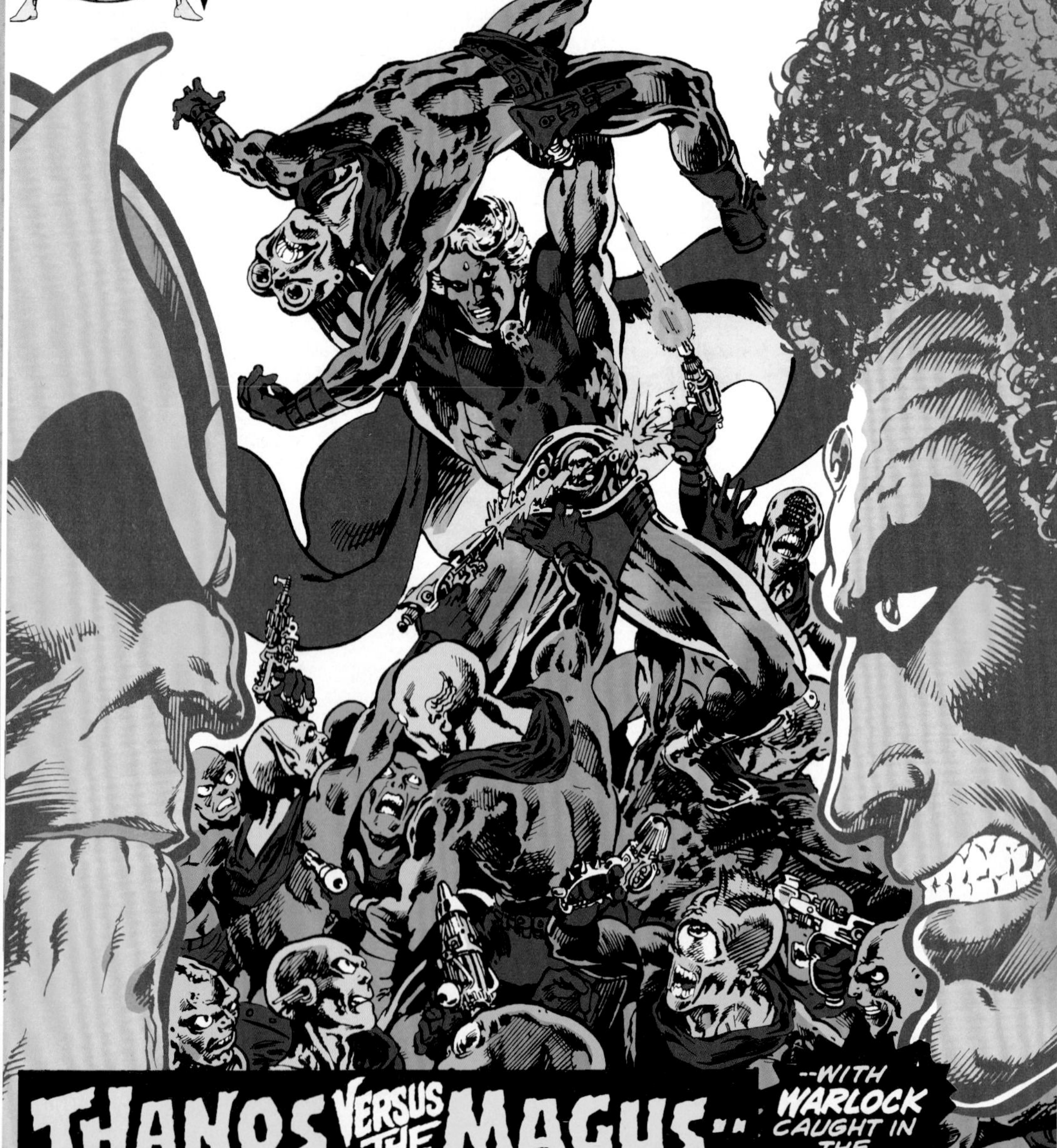

Stan Lee PRESENTS: THE POWER OF WARLOCK! TM
HOW STRANGE MY DESTINY!
PART I CHAPTER I
THE PRICE!
WELCOME TO THE "WHO'S WHO OF OUTER SPACE" DEPT. -- OR -- "HOW CAN YOU TELL THE MONSTERS FROM THE HEROES WITHOUT A PROGRAM?"
ENTERING STAGE CENTER: THE FIRST OF 25,000 RELIGIOUS FANATICS CALLED THE BLACK KNIGHTS OF THE CHURCH OF UNIVERSAL TRUTH! THESE ZEALOTS HAVE BEEN ORDERED BY THE MAGUS, THE GOD THEY WORSHIP, TO KILL EVERYONE THEY FIND IN THIS COMPARTMENT!
OCCUPYING STAGE CENTER THE VICTIMS FROM RIGHT TO LEFT...
GAMORA: THANOS' BEAUTIFUL BUT DEADLY ASSISTANT!
ADAM WARLOCK: OUR HERO, AND A MAN PITTED AGAINST HIS OWN INNER SELF AND THE PEOPLE WHO WORSHIP THAT SELF AS A DEITY!
THANOS: THE DARK TITAN, WHO HAS COME TO WARLOCK'S AID FOR HIS OWN SINISTER PURPOSES!
PIP: A GENERALLY USELESS TROLL!
DEATH TO THE ENEMIES OF OUR LORD!
A WOLFMANSTARLINLEIALOHAORZECHOWSKI PRODUCTION

DESTROY THE INFIDELS!
AWAY FROM ME, YOU CRETINS!
I'LL NOT HAVE BLIND FOOLS SUCH AS YOURSELVES MANHANDLING ME...
I HAVE NEWS FOR YOU, WARLOCK!
...OR THIS GOLDEN SIMPLETON, WHO APPEARS TO HAVE DECIDED TO LIE DOWN AND DIE!
I MAY STILL BE ABLE TO SAVE YOUR GLEAMING HIDE...
...BUT I CANNOT DO IT ALONE. I NEED YOUR HELP!
SO FIGHT! BLAST YOU, FIGHT!
YOU MEAN LIKE THIS?
EXACTLY!
GAMORA!?
I ALREADY STAND BY YOUR SIDE, MASTER!
YOUR LEFT FLANK IS WELL PROTECTED!
EXCELLENT!

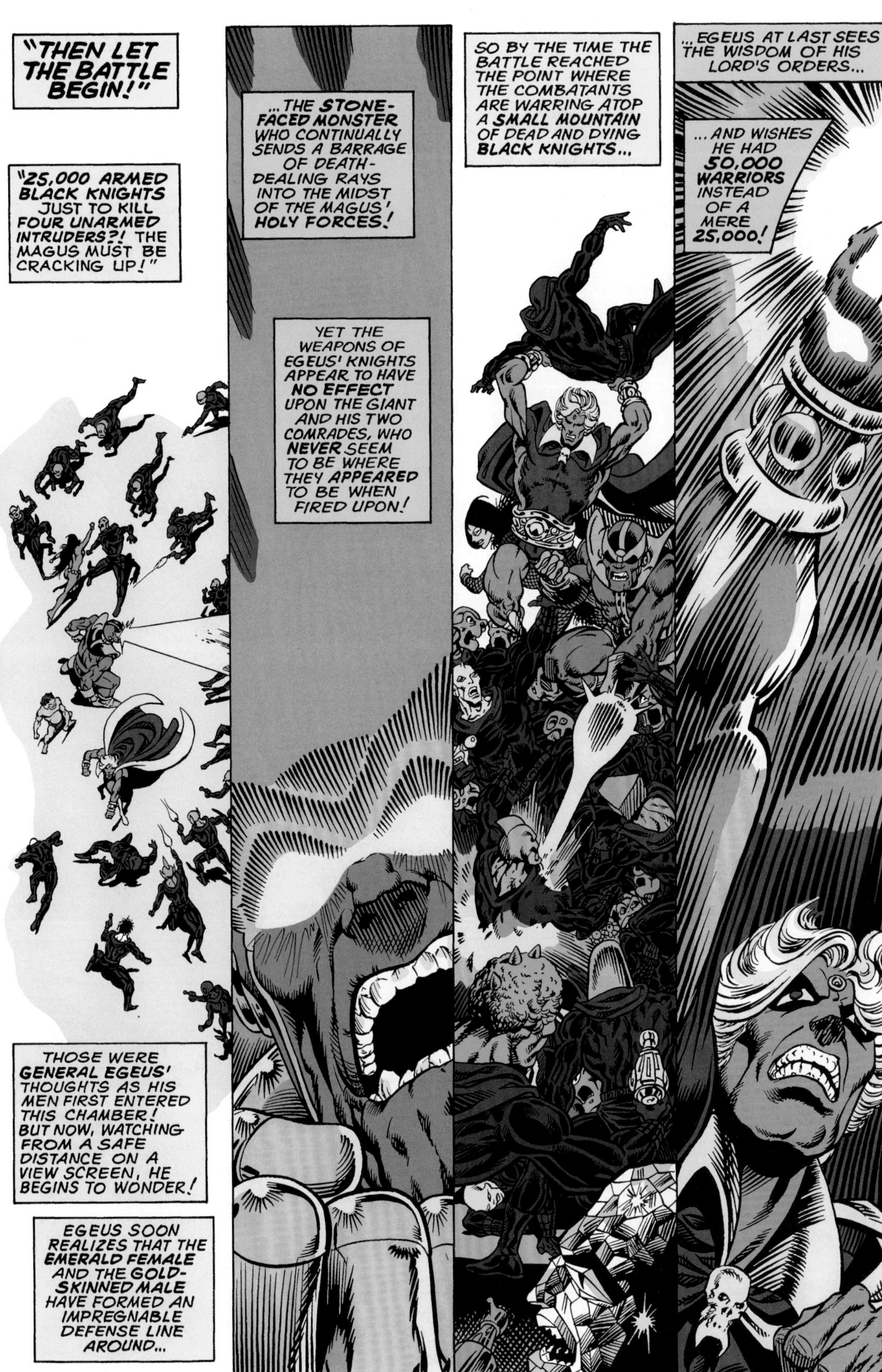
"THEN LET THE BATTLE BEGIN!"
"25,000 ARMED BLACK KNIGHTS JUST TO KILL FOUR UNARMED INTRUDERS?! THE MAGUS MUST BE CRACKING UP!"
THOSE WERE GENERAL EGEUS' THOUGHTS AS HIS MEN FIRST ENTERED THIS CHAMBER! BUT NOW, WATCHING FROM A SAFE DISTANCE ON A VIEW SCREEN, HE BEGINS TO WONDER!
EGEUS SOON REALIZES THAT THE EMERALD FEMALE AND THE GOLD-SKINNED MALE HAVE FORMED AN IMPREGNABLE DEFENSE LINE AROUND...
...THE STONE-FACED MONSTER WHO CONTINUALLY SENDS A BARRAGE OF DEATH-DEALING RAYS INTO THE MIDST OF THE MAGUS' HOLY FORCES!
YET THE WEAPONS OF EGEUS' KNIGHTS APPEAR TO HAVE NO EFFECT UPON THE GIANT AND HIS TWO COMRADES, WHO NEVER SEEM TO BE WHERE THEY APPEARED TO BE WHEN FIRED UPON!
SO BY THE TIME THE BATTLE REACHED THE POINT WHERE THE COMBATANTS ARE WARRING ATOP A SMALL MOUNTAIN OF DEAD AND DYING BLACK KNIGHTS...
...EGEUS AT LAST SEES THE WISDOM OF HIS LORD'S ORDERS...
...AND WISHES HE HAD 50,000 WARRIORS INSTEAD OF A MERE 25,000!

YET ALL THINGS IN THIS UNIVERSE HAVE THEIR LIMIT, AND THAT INCLUDES THANOS' POWER!

SOON THE BATTLE TURNS TO DIRECT HAND-TO-HAND COMBAT, WITH THE MASSIVE TITAN RELEASING BOLTS OF DEATH ONLY WHEN THEIR USE IS ABSOLUTELY NECESSARY!

AND SO...

WARLOCK! THIS SITUATION HAS BECOME UNWORKABLE!

WE MUST RETREAT!

HEAD FOR THE STAIRS!

THIS WAY, THEN!

BOY-O-BOY! AM I GLAD TO GET OUT OF THERE!

I DON'T THINK I COULD HAVE HELD UP OUR REAR GUARD ANY LONGER!

OH REALLY! I MUST HAVE MISSED THAT!

... AND WE LOSE OURSELVES IN THE NIGHT...

BY ORION!

"NOW WHAT?" MOANS PIP!

"WE FIGHT ON UNTIL WE DROP!" RESPONDS WARLOCK!

BUT THANOS RUMBLES, "NO!"

BY THE GREAT SOUL! THE MASTER IS TRAPPED UP THERE!

I FEAR THERE'S NOTHING WE CAN DO FOR HIM, GAMORA! RIGHT NOW WE MUST CONCENTRATE ON TAKING LEAVE OF THIS ROOM!

THANOS CLAIMED THERE YET REMAINED A WAY TO DEFEAT THE MAGUS! IF THAT'S SO, I MUST FIND IT AND RETAIN MY FREEDOM!

UNFORTUNATELY, I'VE LESS THAN 2 1/2 HOURS TO DO THIS IN...
...SO I'M AFRAID THERE CAN BE NO GOING BACK FOR THOSE WHO HAVE FALLEN!

BESIDES, I'VE A FEELING THANOS IS QUITE CAPABLE OF HANDLING THAT SITUATION BACK THERE!
HEY, ADAM! WHERE THE HECK ARE WE?
WE'RE IN THE CAVERNS THAT HONEY-COMB THE AREA AROUND THE HOLY PALACE, MAGGOT!

IN FACT, WE'RE DIRECTLY UNDER THE PALACE RIGHT NOW, IF I'M NOT MISTAKEN!
WHY HAVE WE COME DOWN THIS WAY?
I'M NOT REALLY SURE. I GUESS IT'S PROBABLY THE MOST UNEXPECTED ROUTE, THUS THE SAFEST...
...BUT TO BE HONEST WITH YOU, I'M NOT EVEN SURE HOW I KNOW ABOUT THESE CAVES!

THERE'S SO MUCH I'M NO LONGER SURE OF!
TWO DAYS AGO I WAS CONFIDENT THAT MY MIND AND BODY COULD HANDLE ANY SITUATION THAT COULD HAVE ARISEN!
"I DIDN'T KNOW THAT WHEN I FIRST BATTLED THE MAGUS!
"I DIDN'T BELIEVE IT WHEN I SET OUT TO MAKE HIM PAY FOR MURDERING A YOUNG GIRL BEFORE MY VERY EYES!
"I STILL WOULDN'T ACCEPT IT WHEN I ATTACKED ONE OF THE MAGUS' WARSHIPS AND BEGAN THE WEIRDEST MAN (GOD)-HUNT THE STARS HAVE EVER SEEN!
NOW I REALIZE THAT MY BODY IS NOTHING MORE THAN A USELESS SHELL FOR MY EGO...
...AND MY MIND IS A CESSPOOL OF CORRUPTION THAT WILL SOMEDAY SPAWN THE MAGUS!

I soon found myself facing such worthy foes as *CAPT. AUTOLYCUS* and such hideous monsters as *GRAND INQUISITOR KRAYTOR.* The only thing that saved me from their attacks was my vampire *soul gem* which drained them of their life forces.

Unfortunately this gem failed to protect me from being captured and nearly brainwashed by the *MATRIACH* of the *UNIVERSAL CHURCH OF TRUTH,* I finally escaped this fate by fleeing into the realm of madness, but found this was exactly what the *MAGUS* wished me to do.

It seems that *INSANITY,* or rather an abnormal view of *REALITY* is required before my final metamorphisis into the Magus can be complete.

It was also revealed to me that the harmless radiation the Magus had earlier bathed me in would summons a powerful being called the *IN-BETWEENER* who would imprison me in his dark dimension of *DECEPTIONS* and *MISCONCEPTIONS.*

There, over a Timeless Period, my Transformation would be completed and I would Return to this Actuality *5,000 YEARS* in the Past so to Create the Universal Church and eventually Confront and Defeat my Present Self. I was still trying to Understand all this when *THANOS* Suddenly Appeared and Offered to Aid me but Before I could even Accept we were Attacked by 25,000 Black Knights.

*SEE STRANGE TALES #181. --MARV.

I GUESS WE WERE BOTH DESTINED TO BE LOSERS, ADAM! FOR WE SET IMPOSSIBLE GOALS FOR OURSELVES!
I WANTED TO BE A GODDESS AND YOU WISHED TO SLAY A GOD!
IF ONLY WE HAD REALIZED THAT YOU CAN'T ACCOMPLISH SUCH THINGS ALONE!

I'M AFRAID THE ONLY THING YOU CAN DO PROPERLY BY YOURSELF IS...

...DIE!

I'M SO... SORRY... IF I HAD ONLY KNOWN... I... I WOULD HAVE... HAVE...

...PROBABLY DONE EXACTLY AS I HAVE DONE! ONLY IT WOULD BE MUCH HARDER NOW!
I WOULD HAVE STILL ASKED WHY... NOT SEEING THE TRUTH BEFORE ME ALL THE WHILE!

FOR IT IS MY NATURE TO QUESTION BUT NEVER TO ANSWER!

I NOW REALIZE THAT TO SEEK BUT NEVER FIND IS MY... DESTINY!
THE ONLY THING I DON'T UNDERSTAND IS...

WHY?

WHY MUST LIFE BE SO CRUEL? WHY MUST THERE BE SO MUCH MYSTERY...

...SO MUCH PAIN?

BECAUSE THAT IS THE WAY OF LIFE!
WHO?!

THANOS!!
YES, FOR EVERY ACTION THERE MUST BE A REACTION! WITH EVERY GIVE, A TAKE MUST OCCUR! FOR EVERY PLEASURE, A PAIN MUST BE PAID!

YOU, UNLIKE MYSELF, HAVE CHOSEN THE PATH OF THE LIVING!
YOU MUST LEARN TO BE ONE WITH THIS LIFE OR IT WILL DESTROY YOU, ADAM!
THE ONLY WAY TO DO THIS, IS TO PAY ITS PRICE!
ITS PRICE IS PAIN!

END PART ONE...

GREETINGS, READER, MY NAME IS CAPTAIN MARVEL, AND I'M HERE TO ANSWER THAT QUESTION!

AS YOU MAY OR MAY NOT KNOW, I'VE CROSSED SWORDS WITH THANOS IN THE PAST AND SO KNOW HIM FOR WHAT HE TRULY IS!*

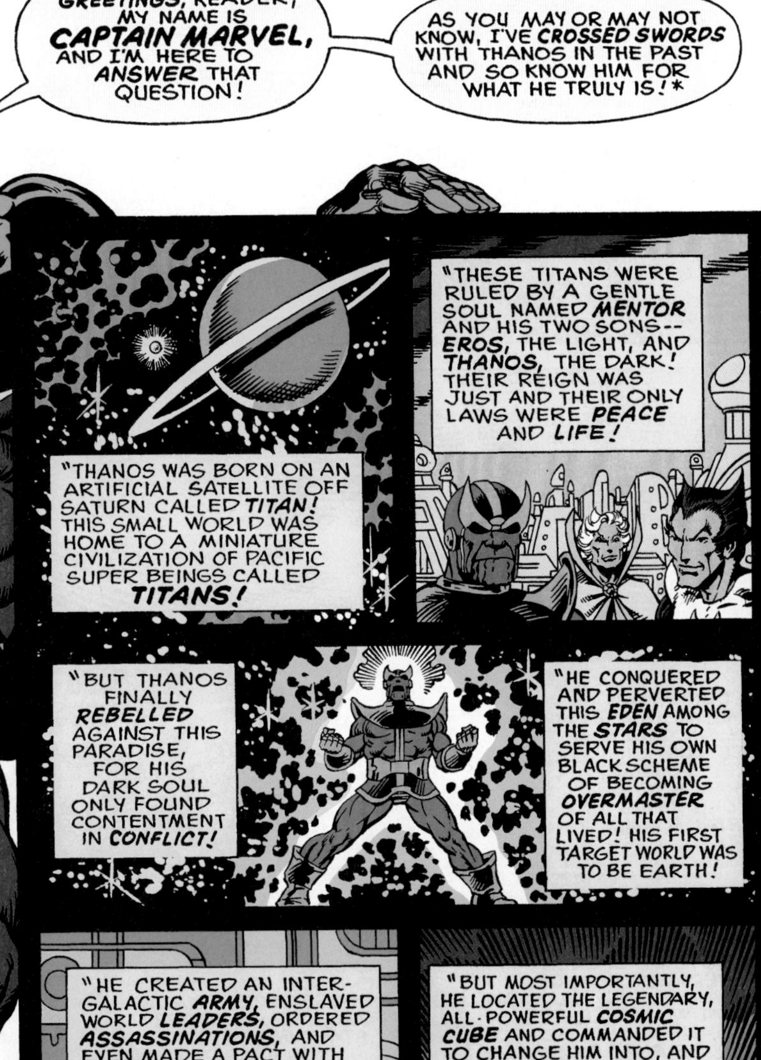

*SEE CAPTAIN MARVEL'S OWN MAG #25-33. --MARV.

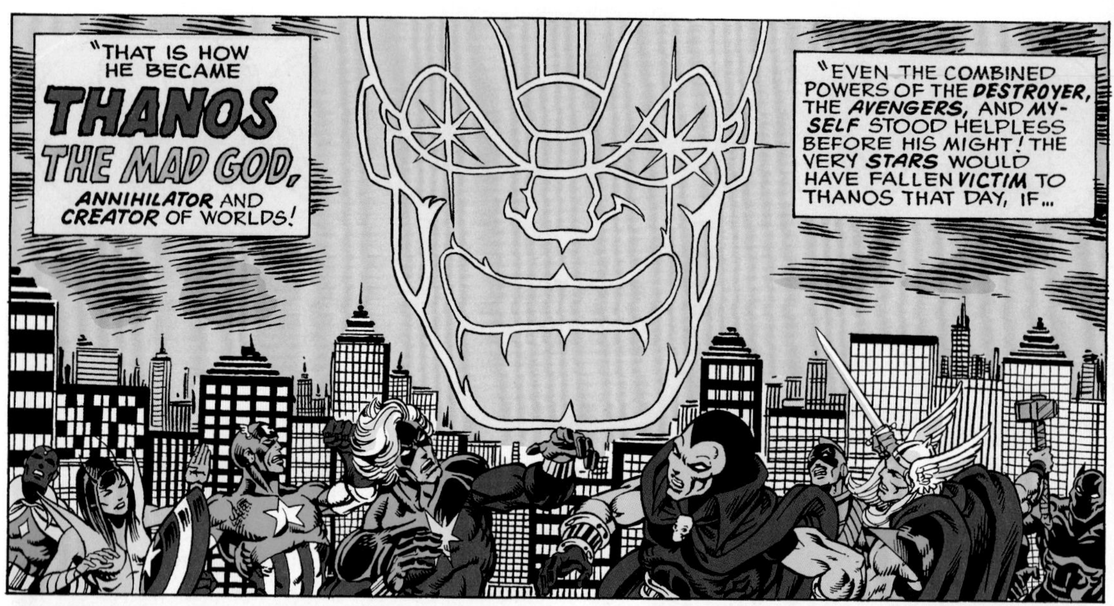
"THAT IS HOW HE BECAME
THANOS
THE MAD GOD,
ANNIHILATOR AND CREATOR OF WORLDS!
"EVEN THE COMBINED POWERS OF THE DESTROYER, THE AVENGERS, AND MYSELF STOOD HELPLESS BEFORE HIS MIGHT! THE VERY STARS WOULD HAVE FALLEN VICTIM TO THANOS THAT DAY, IF...

"...I HADN'T REALIZED THAT HE STILL DERIVED HIS STRENGTH FROM THE COSMIC CUBE! SO I SHATTERED THE CUBE, BELIEVING THAT WOULD ALSO DESTROY THANOS!

"YET UNKNOWN TO ME AT THE TIME, THE CUBE'S DESTRUCTION MERELY FORCED THANOS TO RETURN TO HIS MORTAL FORM...
"...TO SHRINK FROM THE SIZE OF THE UNIVERSE TO THE SIZE OF A MAN FLOATING UNCONSCIOUS AT THE CENTER OF THE UNIVERSE!"

BUT HE'S BACK IN OPERATION NOW, DEAR READER, AND YOU KNOW THAT WHATEVER HE'S PLANNING HAS GOT TO BE PURE EVIL!
SO SIT BACK, RELAX AND ENJOY THE REST OF THIS BOOK, FOR YOU NOW POSSESS SECRET KNOWLEDGE, AND SO UNDERSTANDING IS ALSO YOURS!
MAY YOUR STAR BE AT PEACE!
MEANWHILE, BACK TO OUR STORY...

CHAPTER III
ENTER THE Redemption PRINCIPLE!
AS YOU NOTICED, MENTALLY PHASING MORE THAN ONE-SELF TO ANY LOCALE REQUIRES INTENSE CONCENTRATION THAT IS NOT POSSIBLE AMIDST A BATTLE ROYAL!
THAT IS WHY I WAS FORCED TO KEEP THOSE BLACK KNIGHTS OCCUPIED WHILE YOU ESCAPED, THEN CATCH UP WITH YOU LATER BY LONE PHASING!
HEY!

BY THE WAY, WE ARE NOW WITHIN MY PRIVATE SPACE ARK, IN FREE DRIFT OUTSIDE OF THE GRAVITATIONAL AND DETECTIONAL FIELDS OF THE MAGUS' HOMEWORLD!

I CALL THIS PLACE "SANCTUARY"!

SOME 'SANCTUARY'-- A TROLL COULD GET KILLED IN SUCH A PLACE!

THEN I WOULD ADVISE WEARING THESE METAL BOOTS AND STAYING ON THE MAGNETIZED WALKWAYS!
THIS WILL KEEP YOU FROM DAMAGING ANY OF THE VALUABLE EQUIPMENT I HAVE HERE!
I APPRECIATE THE CONCERN!

I SENSE TREMENDOUS FORCES CONTAINED WITHIN YOUR SANCTUARY, THANOS!
IF THE NEED ARISES... PERHAPS!
AS FOR NOW, IT WILL SERVE AS OUR BASE OF OPERATIONS AGAINST THE MAGUS -- AND NOT HIS WORLD.
PLANET-SHATTERING FORCES... PERHAPS?

SECONDLY, ARE YOU SURE YOU SENSED, RATHER THAN RECOGNIZED, SANCTUARY'S MIGHT?
COULD IT BE... THAT YOU ARE NOW SOMEHOW TAPPING INTO YOUR OWN FUTURE KNOWLEDGE... SENSES YOU'LL NOT FULLY DEVELOP UNTIL YOU BECOME THE MAGUS!
THAT WOULD EXPLAIN YOUR INEXPLICABLE FAMILIARITY WITH THAT MAZE BENEATH THE PALACE!

YES, THAT WOULD RESOLVE ONE MYSTERY, YET MANY QUESTIONS REMAIN TO BE ANSWERED!
SUCH AS, WHY ARE YOU GOING TO ALL THE TROUBLE AND EXPENSE OF AIDING ME?

WOULD YOU BELIEVE I'M DOING ALL THIS OUT OF THE GOODNESS OF MY HEART?

BINGO!
NO, FOR I PERCEIVE THAT YOU HAVE NO HEART!

THAT'S TRUE, I HAVE NO HEART, BUT I'VE DREAMS, AND ONCE HAD A SMALL WORLD I RULED!

BUT MY ENEMIES SHATTERED MY PLANS TO TURN TITAN INTO A TECHNOLOGICAL SUPERWORLD, AND OVERTHREW MY REGIME!

YET THE VISION REMAINS, AND SOMEDAY I SHALL ONCE AGAIN OCCUPY THE THRONE OF POWER UPON TITAN!

TO REBUILD MY DREAM, CERTAIN TOOLS WILL HAVE TO BE USED PROPERLY!
ONE SUCH TOOL WILL BE THIS TIME MACHINE WHICH I HAVE CREATED!
WITH IT, NO MYSTERY MAY REMAIN A SECRET TO ME!

ANOTHER TOOL I SHALL USE TO GAIN MY ENDS WILL BE YOURSELF -- OR, RATHER, YOUR SOUL GEM!
UNFORTUNATELY, MY PLANS CANNOT BE ACTED UPON IMMEDIATELY, AND AS IT STANDS NOW, YOUR FUTURE WILL SOON NEGATE YOUR USE-FULNESS TO ME!
THAT AND THE FACT THAT THE MAGUS HIMSELF MAY SOME-DAY BECOME A THREAT TO MY SCHEMES FORCES ME...

...TO TERMINATE YOUR OTHER SELF'S EXISTENCE, SO THAT IT IS YOU, RATHER THAN THE MAGUS I MUST EVENTUALLY DEAL WITH!

TO DO THIS, I USED "KNOW-LEDGE I," MY TIME PROBE, TO OBSERVE AND CLASSIFY EVERY ASPECT OF YOUR PRESENT AND FUTURE LIFE!

"THIS DATA CONVINCED ME, FOR REASONS BEYOND YOUR GRASP, THAT DIRECT INTER-VENTION WAS UNDESIRABLE!
"SO IT WAS THAT I SET OUT TO CREATE GAMORA, AN AGENT THAT MAY HAVE BEEN CAPABLE OF SLAYING THE MAGUS!"

"I FOUND **GAMORA** SOME YEARS FROM NOW ON A FAR-OFF WORLD WITH HER PEOPLE, THE **ZEN WHOBERIS,** WHO WERE SURROUNDED BY THE MAGUS', **'HOLY FORCES'**!

"THE **ZEN WHOBERIS** WERE/ARE/WILL BE A PEACE-LOVING RACE WHOSE **RELIGIOUS ACTIVITIES** STEMMED FROM REASONS OF **FAITH** ALONE!

"THEY GENTLY BUT FIRMLY **REFUSED** TO CONVERT TO THE UNIVERSAL CHURCH'S BELIEFS, AND SO WERE ORDERED HERDED INTO A VALLEY TO BE **'REINDOCTRINATED'**!

"THE MAGUS' GRAND INQUISITORS THEN **'PURIFIED'** THOSE FOOLISHLY GENTLE PEOPLE WITH THEIR **DEATH-DEALING RAYS!** SO PASSED THE **ZEN WHOBERIS** INTO HISTORY...

"...EXCEPT FOR **GAMORA,** WHOSE NEWLY-CREATED **HATRED** FOR THE MAGUS AND HIS PEOPLE COULD NOW BE MOLDED TO SERVE MY PLANS!

"**I** RAISED GAMORA HERE ON **'SANCTUARY'**, AND, OVER THE YEARS, ENDOWED HER WITH **POWERS** THAT RIVAL YOUR OWN PHYSICAL ABILITIES! FOR, WAS SHE NOT DESTINED TO KILL **YOU?**

"TO REFINE THOSE **GIFTS,** I ALLOWED HER TO EXACT **VENGEANCE** UPON THOSE INQUISITORS WHO WOULD TAKE PART IN HER PEOPLE'S GENOCIDE **YEARS BEFORE** IT EVER OCCURED!

"I HAD HOPED THIS WOULD CREATE A MAJOR-ENOUGH **RIFT** IN THE MAGUS' **CONTINUOUS REALITY** TO ALLOW GAMORA TO **ASSASSINATE** YOUR OTHER SELF BEFORE HE COULD CALL FOR THE IN-BETWEENER!

GENERAL EGEUS, HOW--WITH 25,000 MEN AT YOUR DISPOSAL--DID YOU MANAGE TO LOSE THREE PEOPLE AS CONSPICUOUS AS THEY?

WELL, SIRE, THE ONE CALLED THANOS SIMPLY VANISHED INTO THIN AIR AND...

THANOS!

MY SECRET FOE HAS AT LAST BEEN REVEALED TO ME!

THANOS... OF COURSE! MY INTELLIGENCE SERVICES HAVE WARNED ME OF THIS DEMON BECOMING A POSSIBLE THREAT TO ME SOMEDAY!
PLUS, IT WOULD TAKE A KEEN AND POWERFUL MIND LIKE HIS TO HAVE CONCEIVED THE DIABOLICAL MACHINATIONS THAT HAVE TAKEN PLACE THIS DAY!
YET THANOS HAS NOT PROVEN HIMSELF CLEVER ENOUGH, FOR EVEN THOUGH HE HAS ALTERED MY PAST, IT HAS NOT BEEN ENOUGH TO TERMINATE MY BEING!
TOO DEEPLY ARE MY ROOTS BURIED IN THE CORNERSTONES OF ORDER AND CHAOS FOR A WORSHIPPER OF DEATH, SUCH AS THANOS, TO EFFECT ME!
FOR I AM PURE LIFE AND ONLY I CAN DETERMINE MY FUTURE!

STILL, I BELIEVE IT'S BEST I LOCATE WARLOCK AND THANOS TO AVOID ANY FUTURE TROUBLE! TO DO THIS, I NEED ONLY PLOT THE INBETWEENER'S NEW COURSE AND FOLLOW IT ALONG UNTIL I FIND...

...THANOS' SPACE ARK! THAT'S PECULIAR! ALL OF THANOS' DEFENSE SCREENS ARE DOWN, AS IF THANOS WERE INVITING ME TO SEND FORTH A SPY BEAM, TO EXAMINE THE INNARDS OF HIS 'SANCTUARY', WHERE...

...I FIND THANOS, WARLOCK, AND THAT TROLL STANDING BEFORE WHAT CAN ONLY BE... BY THE POWERS!
IT'S A TIME-PROBE!!

THIS DEVIL, THANOS, IS MORE DANGEROUS THAN I SUPPOSED! WITH BOTH A TIME-PROBE AND WARLOCK WORKING WITH HIM, HE MAY...
GENERAL! SUMMON YOUR DEATH SQUAD!

BUT THIS TIME I SHALL LEAD THEM, FOR THE STAKES HAVE BECOME ASTRONOMICALLY HIGH!
THAT FOOL, WARLOCK, HAS FALLEN INTO THE HANDS OF A DEMON FAR MORE DIABOLICAL THAN I COULD EVER BE!
SO FOLLOW ME, YOU BLOOD-RED ASSASSINS! I'VE WORK FOR YOU THIS DAY!

SLAY ALL YOU MEET WHEN WE ARRIVE AT OUR DESTINATION, SAVE THE INFIDEL WARLOCK!
FOR HE IS MINE!

MEANWHILE, AT THAT DESTINATION...
YOU KNOW THAT I SPEAK THE TRUTH!

USE THAT PORTION OF YOUR MIND THAT YOU'VE GAINED FROM THE MAGUS AND YOU'LL SEE THAT...
...YOUR SUICIDE IS THE ONLY WAY TO DEFEAT YOUR OTHER SELF!
EVEN THEN, YOUR SELF-DESTRUCTION MUST BE CARRIED OUT BY MEANS OF MY TIME-PROBE OR IT WILL BE USELESS!

YES, I BEGIN TO FOLLOW YOUR TRAIN OF THOUGHT. IT'S NOT MY FUTURE PHYSICAL BODY THAT NOW MENACES US, BUT THE VILE ENTITY MY SOUL IS DESTINED TO BECOME!
THIS BEING THE CASE, IT MEANS THAT ONLY I AND I ALONE CAN STOP THE MAGUS' MADNESS!
SO START YOUR TIME VEHICLE, THANOS, FOR ADAM WARLOCK IS NOW PREPARED...
...TO DESTROY HIS OWN SOUL!

NEXT: THE CONCLUSION OF
HOW STRANGE MY DESTINY!
PLUS
THE BIZARRE DEATH OF ADAM WARLOCK!

WARLOCK MARVEL COMICS GROUP™

APPROVED BY THE COMICS CODE AUTHORITY

25¢ CC 11 FEB 02153

WARLOCK™

Stan Lee PRESENTS: THE POWER OF WARLOCK! TM
HOW STRANGE MY DESTINY
PART 2 · CHAPTER 4
ESCAPE INTO THE INNER PRISON!
ONWARD, MY DEATH SQUAD!
SLAY ALL WITHIN THESE WALLS...
...ALL SAVE ADAM WARLOCK, FOR... HE IS MINE!
HOLY GOOSH! IT'S THE MAGUS!
STORY-LAYOUT JIM STARLIN
FINISHED ART STEVE LEIALOHA
LETTERING TOM ORZECHOWSKI
EDITING MARV WOLFMAN

QUESTION: WHAT THE BLAZES IS GOING ON?

WE'VE LEARNED THAT ALL THE DEATH-TRAPS WARLOCK HAS SURVIVED SINCE THEN HAVE BEEN CLEVERLY CONDITIONING ADAM, MENTALLY AND PHYSICALLY, TO BE TRANSMUTED INTO THE EVIL BEING KNOWN AS THE MAGUS.

FORTUNATELY, THIS PLAN HAS RUN INTO A SNAG.

THAT SNAG'S NAME IS THANOS!

THANOS, THE FORMER TYRANT OF TITAN, HAS DECIDED, FOR REASONS OF HIS OWN, TO AID ADAM BY USING HIS TIME-PROBE TO CHANGE THE WARLOCK'S FUTURE-MAGUS' PAST, THUS ALLOWING OUR HERO A CHANCE TO KILL HIMSELF AND AVOID BECOMING THE FIEND HE NOW BATTLES.

... WE'LL JUST HAVE TO FILL IN THE BLANK SPOTS AS WE GO ALONG! -- JIM and MARV.
FOOLS, I, THE MAGUS, HAVE DECREED THAT WARLOCK IS TO BE TAKEN UNHARMED!
I'VE A FATE FAR WORSE THAN DEATH PREPARED FOR HIM!
A FATE THAT WAITS LESS THAN AN HOUR AWAY!

THANOS, HE'S TALKING ABOUT THE IN-BETWEENER, THE BEING THAT'S DESTINED TO CARRY ME OFF TO HIS DARK DIMENSION, WHERE I'LL BE CHANGED INTO THE MAGUS...
... BY THE DARK FORCES OF CHAOS AND ORDER!

ONLY IF THIS WALL OF RELIGIOUS FANATICS BEFORE US PREVENTS US FROM REACHING MY TIME-PROBE.

BUT HOW DO WE GET PAST THEM? THESE ZEALOTS CONTINUE TO POUR IN THROUGH THAT PHASING ENTRANCE THE MAGUS CREATED...
... AND EVEN WORSE, OUR TIME RUNS SHORT!
EXACTLY! THE MAGUS HOPES TO KEEP US BUSY UNTIL THE IN-BETWEENER'S ARRIVAL, WHEN NOTHING WE CAN DO WILL SAVE YOU!
AS IT IS NOW, OUR ONLY HOPE RESTS WITH YOUR...
...SOUL GEM!

NO, NOT THAT!
I DARE NOT USE IT AGAIN!
YOU MUST!
I HAVE NOT THE POWER TO DISPATCH THESE CRETINS AND THEN DO WHAT MUST BE DONE AFTERWARD!

WITH YOUR VAMPIRE GEM YOU CAN DRAIN THE LIFE-FORCES FROM THESE MAGGOTS SO QUICKLY THAT NOT EVEN THE MAGUS WILL BE ABLE TO STOP YOU!

WE CAN THEN USE THE TIME-PROBE TO ELIMINATE THE MAGUS' EXISTENCE COMPLETELY, AND SO SAVE THE STARS FROM EVER FALLING UNDER HIS ENSLAVING YOKE!
BUT... YOU DON'T UNDERSTAND WHAT IT MEANS TO USE THIS DAMNABLE GEM!

THIS JEWEL'S VICTIMS DON'T DIE! THEIR SOULS ARE YANKED FROM THEIR BODIES AND COME TO REST WITHIN MY MIND, TO TORMENT ME FOR ENDING THEIR EXISTENCE!
I JUST CAN'T USE IT AGAIN!
NO MATTER WHAT HAPPENS!

WELL, THEN THINK OF THE TORTURE YOU'LL SUFFER IF YOU ALLOW YOURSELF TO BE TRANSFORMED INTO THE MAGUS!

A SMALL PART OF THAT WHICH IS YOU WILL SURVIVE ON AFTER YOUR METAMORPHOSIS, AND IT WILL BE FORCED TO WITNESS THE EVIL THE MAGUS IS AND WILL BE RESPONSIBLE FOR!

YOU'LL SIT AND WATCH YOUR DEATH SQUAD RIP MY LOVELY ASSISTANT GAMORA APART, LIMB BY LIMB...

...AND YOU'LL SEE YOUR FRIEND PIP SHOT DEAD BEFORE YOUR ONCE AND FUTURE EYES -- AND YOU'LL KNOW YOU COULD HAVE SAVED THEM!
FOR THE SAKE OF THE GREAT COPROLITE!

WILL YOU LISTEN TO OL' ROCK-PUSS?!
NO! I'LL NOT BE FORCED TO USE THIS EMERALD DEVIL AGAIN, NO MATTER WHAT THE COST!

FINE SENTIMENTS, MY GOLDEN SAINT, BUT HAS IT OCCURRED TO YOU JUST WHO WILL PAY FOR YOUR LOFTY CONVICTIONS?
YOU?

NO! IT WILL BE THE MILLIONS OF PEOPLE YOU SHALL ENSLAVE, AS THE MAGUS, WHO WILL PAY!
"LISTEN TO HIM!
IT WILL BE THE THOUSAND WORLDS YOUR UNIVERSAL CHURCH OF TRUTH CONQUERS WHO SHALL PAY FOR YOUR HIGH MORAL STANDARDS.
"YES, LISTEN!
IT WILL BE THE ZEN WHOBRIS YOU GENOCIDE AND THE NON-PRODUCTIVES YOU MASSACRE WHO SHALL FOOT THE BILL FOR YOUR--
NO!
"YES! RELEASE ME!
THERE IS A ROAR AND A FLASH, THEN SUDDENLY WARLOCK REALIZES HE HAS UNLEASHED...
...THE POWER OF THE SOUL GEM!

THE HELL YOU SAY!
YOU'VE JUST PROVEN YOUR SELF WORTHY OF BECOMING THAT WHICH I AM!
HOW?! NO! I DIDN'T MEAN...

YOU SPOUT SANCTIMONIOUS TRIVIA ABOUT HONOR AND GOODNESS...
NO!
...BUT TO GAIN YOUR OWN ENDS YOU'VE JUST SLAUGHTERED A ROOM FULL OF MEN!

YOU'VE AT LAST REVEALED ME TO BE, NOT A PERVERTED VERSION OF YOUR SOUL, BUT RATHER, A TRUE IMAGE!

A TRUE IMAGE THAT'S ABOUT TO SEE THAT YOU NO LONGER INTERFERE WITH WHAT HAS BEEN AND WILL BE!

FORTUNATELY A TRUE IMAGE LIKE TRUTH ITSELF, IS A SUBJECTIVE CONCEPT, ONE TO BE ACCEPTED OR REJECTED DEPENDING ON THE VIEWER'S PREJUDICES, SO...
...MAGUS, I REJECT YOUR TRUTH!
KATOOOOSH!

QUICKLY, WARLOCK, INTO THE TIME PROBE! IT'S PRESET TO TAKE YOU WHERE IT MUST!
BUT ONCE THERE, WHAT SHALL I DO?
THAT YOU SHALL KNOW UPON YOUR ARRIVAL!

ALL KNOWLEDGE YOU REQUIRE RESIDES WITHIN THE MEMORIES YOU'VE BEGUN, OF LATE, TO SHARE WITH THE MAGUS! *
*SEE LAST ISSUE. --M.
HOLD UP A SEC, GOLDY! I THINK WITH YOU THINGS MAY BE...

...SAFER!
WHAT THE DEUCE IS THIS?
IT'S KISMET, PIP!

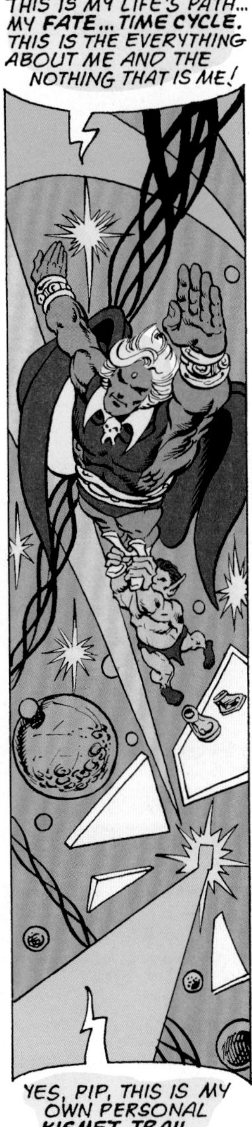
THIS IS MY LIFE'S PATH... MY FATE... TIME CYCLE. THIS IS THE EVERYTHING ABOUT ME AND THE NOTHING THAT IS ME!
YES, PIP, THIS IS MY OWN PERSONAL KISMET TRAIL...

...AND I'M HERE TO DESTROY IT!

I REALIZED BACK ON THANOS' SANCTUARY I THAT THE ONLY WAY TO END THE MAGUS' VILE EXISTENCE IS TO TERMINATE MY OWN NOW TWISTED AND CONFUSED LIFE!
YOU SEE, PIP, THAT'S WHAT I'VE COME HERE FOR! I'M HERE TO COMMIT COSMIC SUICIDE!

MEANWHILE, BACK ON SANCTUARY I...

YOU PLANNED ALL THIS, DIDN'T YOU? THE PROTECTIVE SCREENS BEING DOWN SO I COULD ATTACK... WARLOCK WIPING OUT MY FORCES... RUSHING HIM INTO THE TIME STREAM BEFORE HE COULD TRULY REALIZE WHAT HE'S ABOUT TO DO... IT WAS ALL PLANNED!
WHY!?

BECAUSE YOU ARE A CREATURE OF CHAOS AND ORDER... PURPOSE... LIFE!
SO, BEING A CREATURE OF VAST POWER, YOU MAY SOMEDAY OPPOSE THAT WHICH I WORSHIP!
FOR I AM A DREAMER OF TRANQUILITY... NON-PURPOSE... DEATH!
THEN, IN THAT CASE...

...ALLOW ME TO GRANT YOU A MOST EXQUISITE DEATH!
THOOOM!

THUS, TITAN AND GOD CLASH WHILE, LESS THAN A HEARTBEAT...

...YET MORE THAN AN INFINITY AWAY, THE DESTINY OF THE STARS IS ABOUT TO BE DECIDED BY...
WARLOCK, LOOK!
NO! YOU CAN'T BE HERE ALREADY?!

BUT ALAS, IT IS I... I, WHOSE SOLE REASON FOR EXISTENCE IS TO ABDUCT YOU TO MY DARK, SOUL-NUMBING REALM AND DO WHAT MY MASTERS, CHAOS AND ORDER, HAVE BID ME DO!
FOR, I AM TRULY THEIR IN-BETWEENER!
THEN PREPARE YOURSELF FOR A STRUGGLE OF COSMIC CONSEQUENCE!
FOR AS TWISTED AS THIS LIFE HAS BECOME, IN-BETWEENER, IT YET REMAINS MINE TO CONTROL...
...AND I'LL DIE BEFORE RELINQUISHING THAT POWER!
CHAPTER 5
THE STRANGE DEATH OF ADAM WARLOCK!

THERE WILL BE NO STRUGGLE, ADAM WARLOCK!
CONFLICT IS NOT THE WAY OF THE IN-BETWEENER. I LEAVE SUCH THINGS TO THOSE WHO WALK THE CORRIDORS OF REALITY OR ILLUSION.
I AM ONE APART FROM SUCH NOTIONS.
FORTUNATELY, I AM NOT!

LET US SEE HOW "ONE APART" HANDLES HAVING HIS SOUL RIPPED LOOSE FROM HIS BODY!

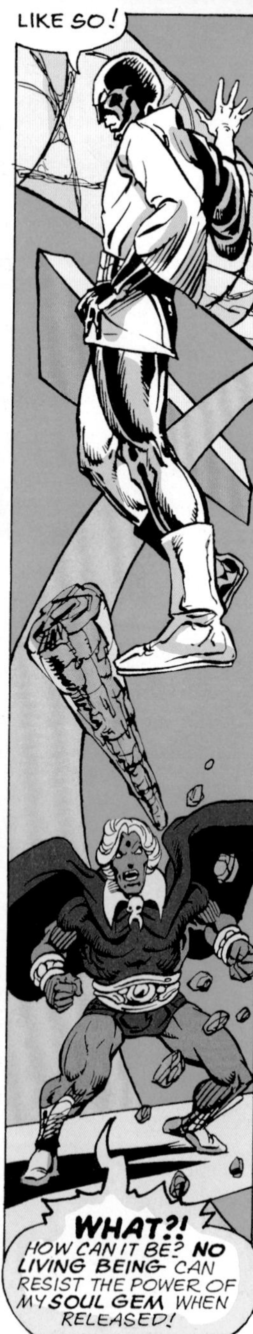
LIKE SO!
WHAT?! HOW CAN IT BE? NO LIVING BEING CAN RESIST THE POWER OF MY SOUL GEM WHEN RELEASED!

YET I CAN, FOR I AM TRULY THE IN-BETWEENER, HE WHO WALKS BETWIXT ALL CONCEPTS SUCH AS...
LIFE AND DEATH... REALITY AND ILLUSION... GOOD AND EVIL... LOGIC AND EMOTION... GOD AND MAN...
ALL THESE THINGS DO I KNOW AND CAN EFFECT, YET NEVER DO THEY TOUCH ME!

THEN YOU WON'T MIND MY TESTING THIS LITTLE THEORY OF YOURS...

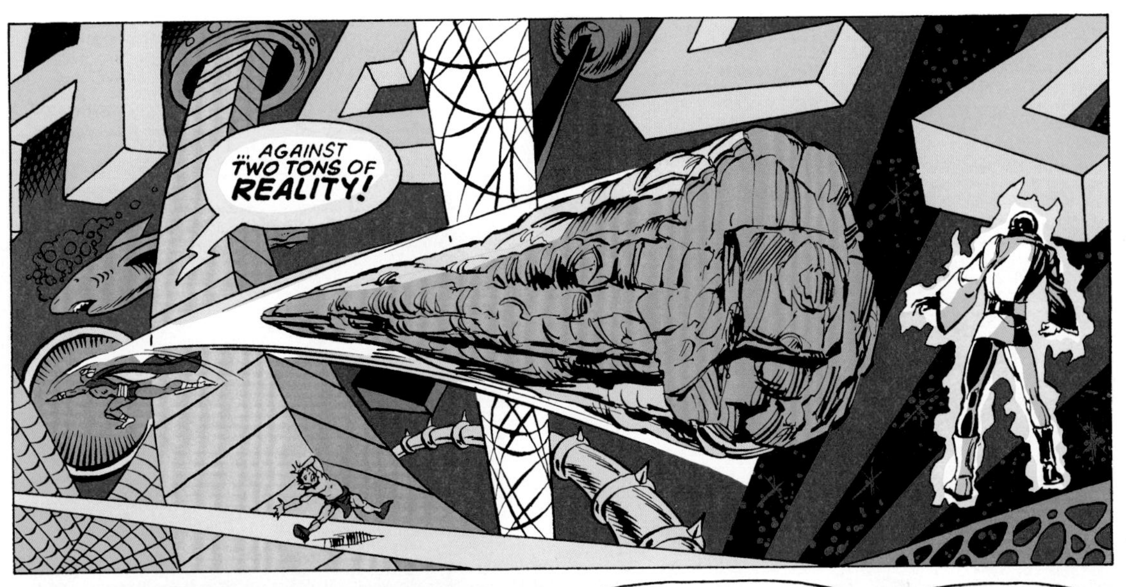
...AGAINST TWO TONS OF REALITY!

NOT AT ALL, FOR AS I'VE SAID, I PASS AMIDST, YET AM NEVER CURSED BY, EMOTION!
STILL, I SENSE YOUR HATRED FOR WHAT I AM ABOUT TO DO, AND SINCE YOU ARE, IN EFFECT, THE SOLE CAUSE FOR MY BEING, I WISH TO ASSURE YOU THAT ALL IS NOT AS DARK AS YOU MIGHT SUPPOSE!
I DO THIS, NOT FOR EMOTIONAL REASONS, BUT RATHER, TO MAKE THAT WHICH IS TO COME TRANSPIRE IN A MORE ORDERLY FASHION!
YOU SEE, ALL THAT HAS AND WILL OCCUR HAS HAD A NOBLE PURPOSE BEHIND IT!

THERE HAS BEEN, AND ALWAYS SHOULD BE, A STRUGGLE BETWEEN LIFE AND DEATH!
AS IT STANDS NOW, LIFE HAS NEED OF A CHAMPION TO DEFEND ITS CAUSE AGAINST A RECENTLY-ARRIVED AND POWERFUL ADVOCATE OF DEATH!

THE MAGUS, AS STRANGE AS IT MAY SEEM TO YOU, IS TO BE THE CHAMPION OF LIFE!
SO DWELL ON WHAT I HAVE CHOSEN TO REVEAL TO YOU AND, HOPEFULLY, IT SHALL GIVE YOU SOME PEACE IN THESE FINAL FIVE MINUTES YOU ARE DESTINED TO HAVE, IN THIS SPHERE!

DID YOU SAY... FIVE MINUTES!?

YES, IN **FIVE SHORT MINUTES** THE IN-BETWEENER SHALL CARRY WARLOCK OFF TO HIS MAD REALM, AND MY **EXISTENCE** -- AND YOUR **DOOM** -- SHALL BE ASSURED!

OF THIS I FEEL SECURE, FOR THOUGH YOU'VE PROJECTED HIM INTO OUR OWN **TIME CENTER**, WARLOCK WILL NOT HAVE THE **TIME** OR **KNOWLEDGE** TO CHANGE OUR DESTINY!--

--A DESTINY DESIGNED SO THAT **YOU** AND **I** MIGHT CLASH!

FOR I NOW REALIZE THAT YOU ARE THE **CHAMPION OF DEATH** I WAS CREATED TO BATTLE!

EXACTLY! I HAD ORIGINALLY HOPED TO STOP YOU **BEFORE** YOU EVER EXISTED, BY HAVING WARLOCK ABORT YOUR CREATION. I WOULD THEN HAVE BEEN ABLE TO **SLAY** YOUR FAR-LESS-POWERFUL OTHER SELF AT MY **LEISURE**!

BUT AS IT TURNS OUT, I BELIEVE **PERSONALLY** CRUSHING YOU SHALL PROVE MUCH MORE **SATISFYING**!

YOU SPOUT **FUTILE BRAVADO**, MY CRAGGY FOE!

SURELY YOU MUST **REALIZE** I WAS CREATED TO BE YOUR **SUPERIOR**...

...CREATED TO HALT YOUR MAD SCHEME OF **TOTAL STELLAR GENOCIDE**!

MY SUPERIOR? **NEVER!**

FOR I AM **THANOS!**

"I AM DEATH!"

MEANWHILE, AT THE OPPOSITE END OF SANCTUARY I'S VAST INTERIOR...

AND, BACK ON WARLOCK'S KISMET TRAIL...

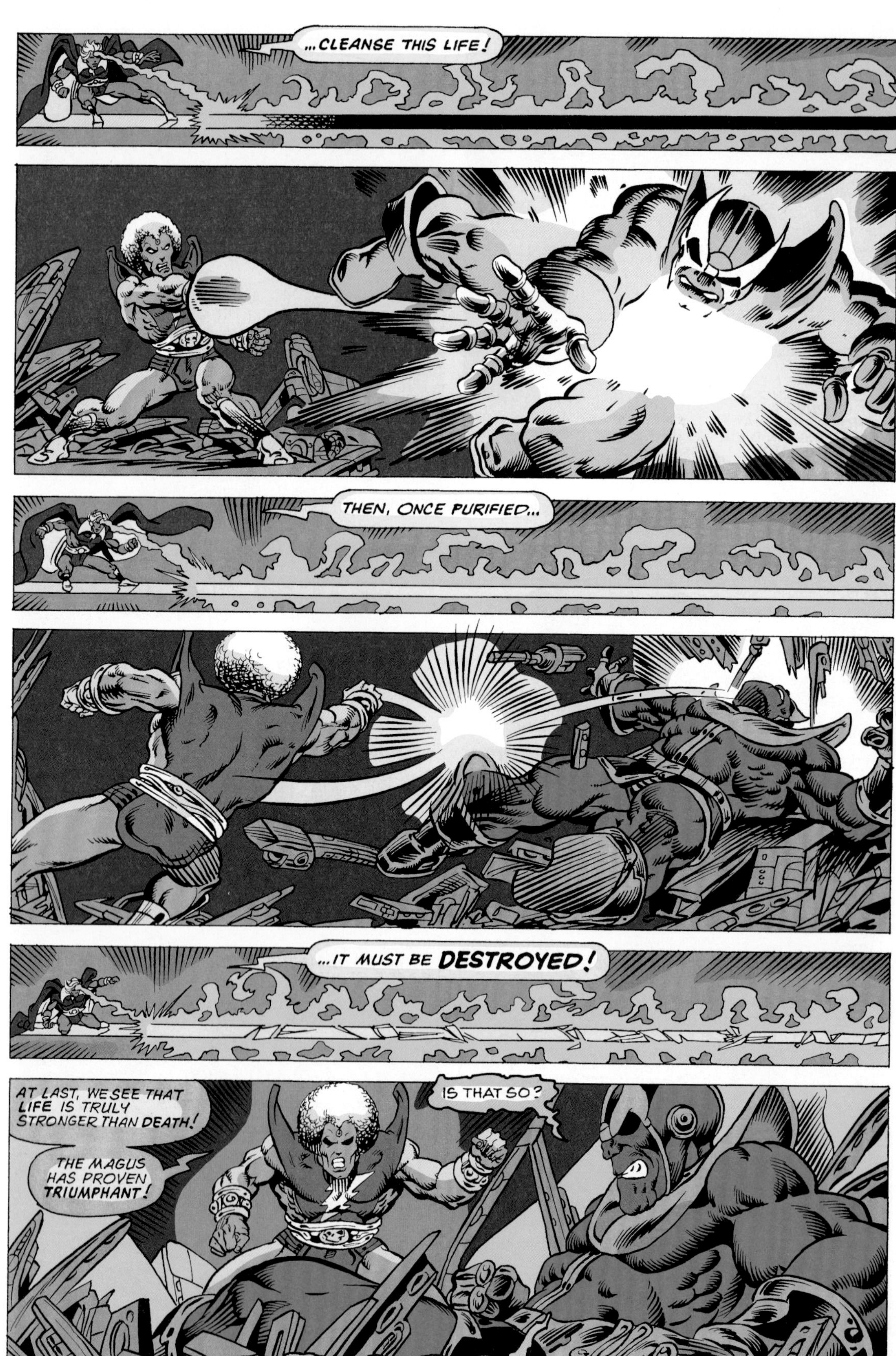
...CLEANSE THIS LIFE!
THEN, ONCE PURIFIED...
...IT MUST BE DESTROYED!
AT LAST, WE SEE THAT LIFE IS TRULY STRONGER THAN DEATH!
THE MAGUS HAS PROVEN TRIUMPHANT!
IS THAT SO?
I SUGGEST YOU LOOK AGAIN, MAGUS!

THE **IN-BETWEENER** MECHANICALLY STEPS FORWARD TO DO WHAT HE HAS BEEN CREATED TO DO! **THANOS** ROARS VILE LAUGHTER AS THE **MAGUS** BEGINS A FUTILE DASH TOWARD THE **TIME PROBE** TO INTERCEPT **WARLOCK**, WHO NOW RACES ALONG THE **SHORTEST** OF HIS LIFE'S PATHS!

ADAM RECALLS **THANOS'** WORDS: "IT IS NOT YOUR **LIFE**, BUT RATHER YOUR **SOUL**, WHICH IS DESTINED TO BECOME OUR **FOE!**" THE MAGUS' PATH HAS BEEN DESTROYED, AND NOW A **NEW LIFE** MUST BE CHOSEN BEFORE THE **IN-BETWEENER** CAN REACH AND THWART ALL ADAM HAS ACCOMPLISHED!

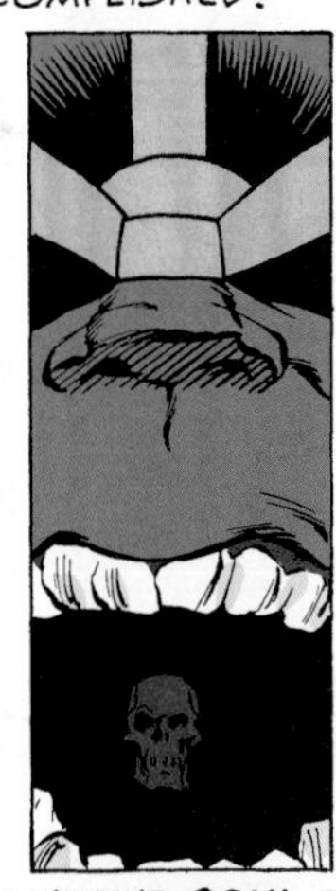

BUT THE MOST **IMPORTANT TASK** YET TO BE ACCOMPLISHED IS INSURING THAT THE **SOUL** OF THIS NEW LIFE IS NOT ALLOWED TO BE **PERVERTED** INTO A FUTURE **MAGUS! THIS** SHALL PROVE TO BE THE **MOST DIFFICULT PART!**

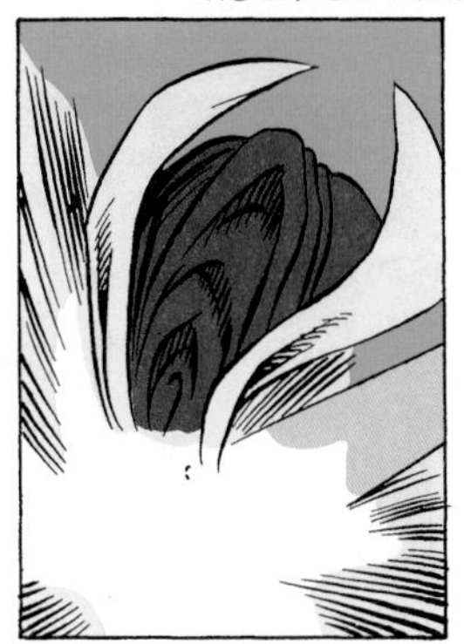

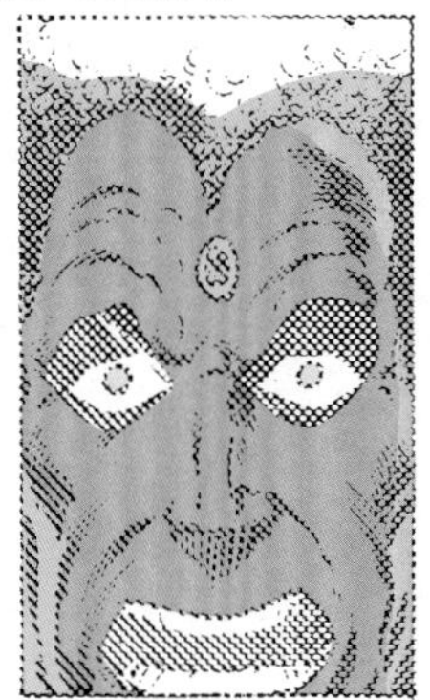

SOMEWHERE... A YEAR -- MAYBE TWO YEARS -- IN THE FUTURE!

"THEN TO BE **REBORN** AGAIN, WITHOUT THE DARK STAIN OF THE **MAGUS** HAVING EVER MARKED IT!

MEANWHILE, BACK AT, OF ALL PLACES, THE PLANET CALLED HOMEWORLD...
BACK TO REALITY, YIPEE! I GUESS!

YES, PIP, BACK TO A UNIVERSE THAT'S NEVER KNOWN A MAGUS OR A UNIVERSAL CHURCH OF TRUTH!
BUT AS I SUSPECTED, IT WOULD APPEAR THAT IF YOU DESTROY ONE FALSE GOD THAT MEN WORSHIP, IT WILL NOT BE LONG BEFORE...

...THEY FIND ANOTHER TO BOW TO!
WELL AIN'T THAT A KICK IN THE...

AWW... THE DEVIL WITH IT ALL, AT LEAST IT AIN'T YOU THIS TIME!
WHAT SAY WE GO ON DOWN TO MAMA ALPHA'S! I'LL BUY YOU A MUG OF AMBROSIAN WINE--
--AND TREAT MYSELF TO A STINGER AND A REVERSED BOWL OF GRUD!

IMPOSSIBLE! NOT HER!

ADAM, YOU COMING?
HEY, WHO WAS THAT? SOMEONE YOU KNOW?

NO, NO ONE REALLY, JUST A MEMORY!

LET'S GO HAVE THAT DRINK, PIP!
I COULD USE IT!

NEXT ?

Warlock soon returned to Earth, but found that he was now far larger than the sun. Shocked, Warlock realized that his immense growth had been caused by spending time in a section of the universe that was expanding faster than Earth's.

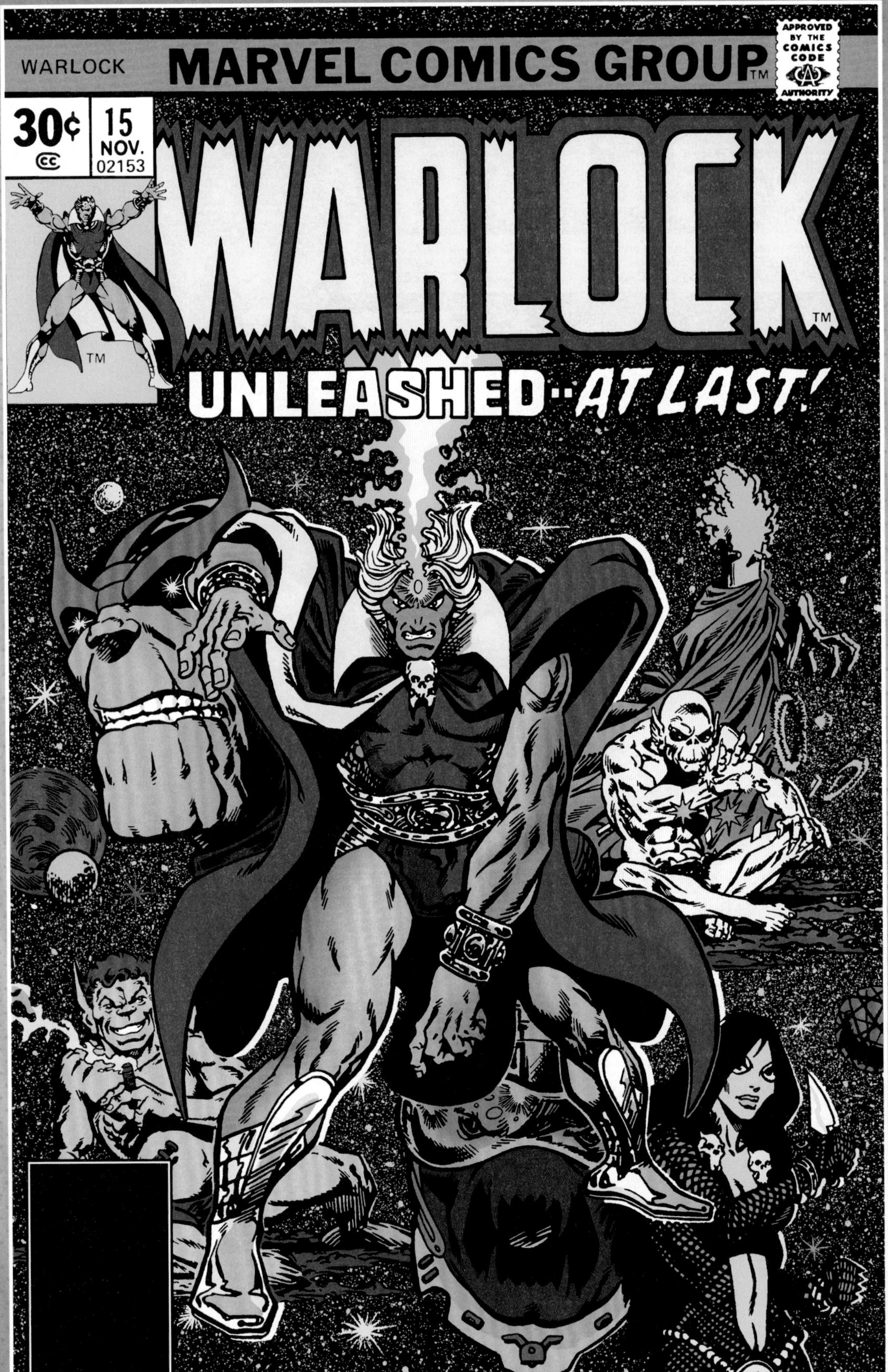

Born to be Earth's man of the future, then forced to abandon his native planet because of his alien ways, he wanders the stars seeking **LIFE!** Gifted with ultra-strength, paranormal reflexes and perceptions, the power of levitation and the curse of a vampire soul-gem, he stands uniquely **ALONE** among the heavens.

Stan Lee PRESENTS: THE POWER OF WARLOCK!™

JUST A SERIES OF EVENTS!

THE **FIRST** OF THESE EVENTS TAKES PLACE IN OUR OWN STAR-SYSTEM OF **SOL**, WHERE WE FIND OUR HERO, **ADAM WARLOCK**, MOST SINGULARLY DISTRESSED.

WHY?

WHY HAVE THE FATES SO CONSPIRED AGAINST **ME**?

BEFORE ME RESTS THE STAR OF MY BIRTH, AND MY HOMEWORLD **EARTH**.

YET, AS CLOSE AS IT IS, **TELLUS** IS NOW FOREVER BEYOND MY REACH.

I CAN **NEVER** AGAIN GO **HOME**!

JY315

EDITOR-ARCHIE GOODWIN / LETTERING-TOM ORZECHOWSKI / COLORING-MICHELE WOLFMAN
ONCE AGAIN TRAPPED INTO DOING EVERYTHING ELSE- **JIM STARLIN**

DURING THE PAST FEW YEARS I'VE WANDERED THOUSANDS OF LIGHT-YEARS FROM EARTH AND HAVE GROWN...
UNFORTUNATELY, MY WORLD HAS NOT GROWN AS QUICKLY.
IT'S FUNNY HOW SOMETHING I'D NEVER HEARD OF, 'THE EXPANDING UNIVERSE THEORY', COULD SO AFFECT ME.
HOW WAS I TO GUESS THAT THE HERCULEAN GALAXY AND ALL IN IT WOULD EXPATIATE AT A RATE FAR SURPASSING THE MILKY WAY'S OWN GROWTH.
NOW I FIND MY SELF A NEBULOUS GIANT AFFECTING NEITHER LIGHT NOR GRAVITY IN THE MINI-SOLAR-SYSTEM BEFORE ME.

ON THE FAR SIDE OF THE SUN, JUST OPPOSITE EARTH... COUNTER-EARTH* LIES.
THERE! THAT MOTE!
*COUNTER-EARTH: THE NEAR-EXACT REPLICA OF EARTH CREATED BY THE HIGH EVOLUTIONARY, AND ONE-TIME ADOPTED PLANET OF ADAM WARLOCK. --ARCHIE

THE PLANET I ONCE CALLED HOME--
DENIED TO ME!

ALL THE PEOPLE I KNEW THERE...
...MIGHT AS WELL BE DEAD--!

--INCLUDING THE ONE BEING WHO MIGHT HAVE AN ANSWER TO MY PREDICAMENT! THE HIGH EVOLUTIONARY!
HE ALWAYS CONSIDERED THIS PLANET AN EXPERIMENT GONE WRONG!
BUT... HE PROMISED HE WOULD SPARE THIS WORLD IF I COULD FREE IT FROM THE EVIL THAT INFESTED IT.

THE PEOPLE OF COUNTER-EARTH THOUGHT ME A GOD SENT TO RESCUE THEM FROM THE VILE CLUTCHES OF THE MAN-BEAST.
I SUCCEEDED! I WAS THEIR... SAVIOR! BUT NOW... I AM AS NOTHING TO THEM.
NOW I NO LONGER EXIST IN THEIR REALITY!
NOW THE GOD IS DEAD.
IN HIS PLACE REMAINS ONLY A HOMELESS MISFIT WHO NO LONGER BELONGS IN THIS STAR SYSTEM.

SO I NOW TAKE LEAVE OF ALL THAT IS MEMORY, AND SET OUT SEARCHING FOR A NEW PLANET I CAN CALL...
... HOME.

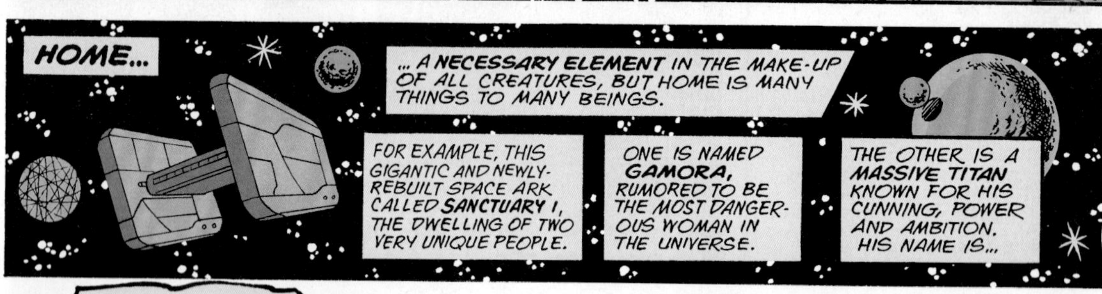
HOME...
... A NECESSARY ELEMENT IN THE MAKE-UP OF ALL CREATURES, BUT HOME IS MANY THINGS TO MANY BEINGS.
FOR EXAMPLE, THIS GIGANTIC AND NEWLY-REBUILT SPACE ARK CALLED SANCTUARY I, THE DWELLING OF TWO VERY UNIQUE PEOPLE.
ONE IS NAMED GAMORA, RUMORED TO BE THE MOST DANGER-OUS WOMAN IN THE UNIVERSE.
THE OTHER IS A MASSIVE TITAN KNOWN FOR HIS CUNNING, POWER AND AMBITION. HIS NAME IS...

THANOS!
I'M BORED.
YES, IT IS A PITY YOU CAN'T AID ME IN MY WORK.
STILL, THERE MUST BE SOME-THING YOU MIGHT DO...
YOU'VE YOUR PRECIOUS MACHINES TO PUTTER WITH CONSTANTLY WHILE I'VE NOTHING TO KEEP ME OCCUPIED, SAVE WATCHING YOU--
--AND, TO BE QUITE FRANK, THAT'S BORING!
OF COURSE...
BUT, REGRETTABLY, I BRED YOU FOR PHYSICAL PROWESS AND NOT SCIENTIFIC ABILITY.

WARLOCK!

AS YOU KNOW, I'VE USE FOR THAT **GLEAMING FOOL** IN MY FUTURE PLANS... THAT'S WHY WE AIDED HIM IN HIS BATTLE AGAINST THE **MAGUS**.*

THAT IS WHY I THINK IT ADVISABLE FOR YOU TO SEEK HIM OUT AND BECOME HIS **UNOFFICIAL BODYGUARD.**

FOR WARLOCK IS **IMPETUOUS** AND **IDEALISTIC**, A COMBINATION WHICH MAY CAUSE HIS **DEATH**...

... UNLESS A **COOLER MIND**, SUCH AS YOUR OWN, IS PRESENT TO SUPPLY, AT TIMES, MUCH-NEEDED **LOGICAL THINKING**.

THIS SHOULD PROVE AN **INTERESTING ASSIGNMENT.** I'LL DEPART AT ONCE.

YES... A MOST INTERESTING ASSIGNMENT.

*SEE ISSUES 9-11.-- ROY.

MY PAST CONTACT WITH THIS ADAM WARLOCK HAS PROVEN HIM TO BE AN INTRIGUING INDIVIDUAL... ALMOST A **SECRET** WRAPPED WITHIN AN **ENIGMA**...

... AND IF THERE'S ANYTHING I REALLY LOVE, IT'S A **MYSTERY**.

SHE IS GONE.

EXCELLENT.

NOW I MAY WORK TOWARD THE **TRUE GOAL** OF MY LABORS WITHOUT HAVING TO CONCEAL THEM FROM EVEN THE ETERNALLY FAITHFUL GAMORA.

SHE WOULD **TURN ON ME** IF SHE KNEW WHAT I AM REALLY STRIVING FOR IS...

...TOTAL STELLAR GENOCIDE...

...AND THAT **WARLOCK** IS THE PAWN THAT WILL MAKE IT ALL **POSSIBLE!**

UNFORTUNATELY, ADAM WARLOCK HAS NEVER HEARD OF THIS PRACTICE.
UNHAND THAT OLD MAN, SPACE SPAWN.
BY THE STARS! I'M SAVED!
THAT'S NOT VERY LIKELY, YOU OLD GEEZER!
NOT WHILE I CAN BLAST THIS GOLDEN TWERP INTO NEXT... ARG!!
YOU'LL DO NOTHING!
FOR LIKE YOUR LUMBERING COMRADE BEHIND ME...
...YOU'LL SOON BE INCAPABLE OF ANYTHING!

WELL, THAT SETTLES THAT.
I DIDN'T WANT TO HANDLE THE SITUATION IN SUCH A MANNER, BUT THE WAY THOSE HULKS WERE MANHANDLING-- YOU, I FEARED YOUR SPACESUIT WOULD BE RUPTURED.
NOW WHAT'S THIS ALL ABOUT, OLD-TIMER?
I BELIEVE I CAN ANSWER THAT.

MY NAME IS MARR GAR!
I AM A CERTIFIED REPRESENTATIVE OF INTER-PLANETEUR INC.
INTERPLANETEUR, INC, IS A MAJOR INTERGALACTIC CORPORATION.

THIS PROSPECTOR, LAMILM GOR, ACQUIRED A LOAN FROM OUR COMPANY FOR 5,000 CR.
A GOODLY SUM, I TAKE IT?

YES, THAT'S WHY WE ASKED THAT LAMILM GOR PUT UP HIS SPACE CRUISER AS COLLATERAL, SO THAT IN THE EVENTUALITY...

...THAT HE FAILED TO MAKE PAYMENT, AS HE DID, WE WOULD REPOSSESS HIS CRAFT, AS WE ARE NOW DOING.
I MEANT TO PAY.
THINGS HAVE BEEN TIGHT.
PLEASE, NO SOB STORIES.

BUT TELL ME, NOW THAT YOU'VE REPOSSESSED HIS CRUISER, WHAT ABOUT THE OLD MAN?
DO YOU TAKE HIM WITH YOU?
WHY, NO!

OUR JOB IS TO REPOSSESS SPACE SHUTTLES. WE HAVE NO LEGAL RESPONSIBILITY TO SUPPLY FREE TAXI SERVICE AFTERWARDS.

OLD MAN, GET IN YOUR CRUISER AND PREPARE TO TAKE OFF...
... AND WHEN YOU ARRIVE AT YOUR DESTINATION, I WOULD SUGGEST YOU SECURE THE FUNDS YOU OWE THESE BEINGS IMMEDIATELY.
NEXT TIME I MAY NOT BE HERE TO SEE THAT YOU'RE NOT ABANDONED IN INTERGALACTIC SPACE.

NOW GO!
NO ONE WILL SEEK TO STOP YOU.
CORRECT?
ULP! CORRECT!

MARR GAR, I'VE MET YOUR KIND OF CREATURE BACK ON EARTH, PASSIONLESS DEALERS OF DOLLARS AND CENTS.

I HAD HOPED YOUR SPECIES WAS RESTRICTED TO THAT SAD PLANET. INSTEAD, I FIND YOUR MADNESS INFESTING THE HEAVENS.

NEVER AGAIN WILL THE STARS SHINE AS BRIGHTLY FOR ME.

WHILE, ELSEWHERE AMONG THOSE STARS, ANOTHER MINI-SPACE-CRAFT CUTS ITS WAY THROUGH THE ETHER.
WELL GAMORA, YOU SET NO SMALL JOB FOR YOURSELF WHEN YOU DECIDED TO...
... HUNT DOWN A STAR-HOPPER LIKE WARLOCK IN THE MIDST OF UNTOLD MILLIONS OF CUBIC LIGHT YEARS OF SPACE.
STILL, IT SHOULD BE WORTH IT.
FOR THIS MAY GIVE ME A CHANCE TO FATHOM HOW WARLOCK FITS INTO MY MASTER'S PLANS...
... PLANS THANOS HAS INTENTIONALLY KEPT ME IN THE DARK ABOUT.
I'M DEEPLY INDEBTED TO THANOS.
IN FACT, I OWE HIM MY LIFE.
YET HIS DEALINGS AND SECRETIVE WAYS RAISE GRAVE DOUBTS WITHIN ME.
WHAT SKULL-DUGGERY IS THANOS UP TO?
WAIT... WHAT'S THIS?
GAMORA, THRALL OF THANOS, I HAVE COME FOR YOU!
NO!
NOT YOU!
TA-BOOM!
THE AIR RINGS WITH GAMORA'S UNBELIEVING CRY, FOLLOWED BY THE EXPLOSIVE SOUND OF TEARING METAL AND BREAKING GLASS.
THEN THE AIR ESCAPES THROUGH THE WRECKED HULL AND ALL THAT IS LEFT IS...

...DEADLY SILENCE.
THE SILENCE OF A DEAD WORLD.
ONCE THIS PLANET TEEMED WITH LIFE, BEFORE IT LEFT ITS STELLAR ORBIT AND BECAME A WANDERER...
...A RUNAWAY PLANET...
...A DRIFTING, DEAD WORLD.
MAGNIFICENT... YET EMPTY.
MUCH THE SAME AS MY OWN LIFE.
I'VE HAD EVERYTHING A PERSON COULD WISH FOR...
...POWER, FREEDOM, FOLLOWERS, EXCITEMENT, EVEN TRUTH.
EVERYTHING EXCEPT PURPOSE.
BACK WHEN I WAS ACTING AS EARTH'S AND COUNTER-EARTH'S PROTECTOR, I HAD A REASON FOR EXISTING, BUT THOSE DAYS ARE PAST.
IN FACT, RECENTLY THE ONLY THING I'VE HAD TO PROTECT ANYONE FROM IS...
...MYSELF.
PERHAPS I SHOULD FIND SOME CAUSE TO CHAMPION, EXCEPT I'VE BECOME TOO CYNICAL OF LATE TO BELIEVE IN ANYTHING.
IT'S DIFFICULT TO STAND UP FOR APATHY!
SO WHAT DO I DO NOW?
PERHAPS YOU SHOULD TRY LOOKING PAST YOURSELF.
WHO?!

MERELY AN ANCIENT TRAVELER... OR PERHAPS A HUMBLE THINKER... MAYBE EVEN A CRAZED HERMIT. THE CHOICE IS YOURS.
JUST AS IT'S YOUR DECISION WHETHER YOU AT LAST UNDERSTAND THAT WHAT YOU SEEK STANDS BEFORE YOU...
...OR CONTINUE TO SHOUT BLINDLY INTO THE WIND.
THEN SPEAK, ANCIENT ONE.

WHAT IS THE PURPOSE I EXIST TO FULFILL?
LIFE IS ITS OWN PURPOSE.
FOR LIFE, LIKE A VIBRATION IN THE AIR, IS A CONSTANTLY EXPANDING FORCE... REACHING OUT... GROWING...
... UNTIL A SECOND VIBRATION COMES UPON IT.
THEY MEET AND AFFECT EACH OTHER.
THERE IS THEN CHANGE.

YET STILL THEY CONTINUE TO EXTEND THEM-SELVES, STRETCH-ING OUT TO THE STARS...
... WHERE THEY'LL FIND NEW CONTACT AND ETERNAL CHANGE.
IS THAT NOT PURPOSE ENOUGH FOR EXISTING... TO BE PART OF THE ALL?
NO!
I WANT MORE.

FOR I HAVE SEEN THE FUTURE AND KNOW I'VE LESS THAN A YEAR TO LIVE.
I WANT TO LEAVE BEHIND SOME-THING OF VALUE.
YOU WISH TO BE REMEMBERED?

YOU WISH TO GAIN, THROUGH MEMORY, THE IMMORTALITY YOUR BIOLOGY DENIES YOU?
WHY DOES ONE SO GIFTED STRIVE FOR SUCH A MEANINGLESS PRIZE?
CAN YOU NOT SEE THAT SUCH A GOAL DIES WITH THE FLESH?

IS IT A FEAR OF DEATH THAT SO BLINDS YOU?

NO, DEATH HOLDS NO TERROR FOR ME.
IT'S LIFE I FEAR.
I'VE NO WISH TO BE ITS VICTIM.

BUT I FEAR THAT IS TO BE YOUR DESTINY, FOR I TOO HAVE SEEN YOUR FUTURE.

AT THIS GAME CALLED LIFE, YOU SHALL PROVE A LOSER.
FOR IT'S YOUR NATURE TO LOSE.
IN LITTLE OVER A YEAR...

... YOU SHALL DIE ALONE, KILLED BY BOTH THANOS' AND YOUR OWN HANDS.
BUT EVEN BEFORE THEN YOU SHALL WATCH GAMORA, PIP, AND MANY OTHERS YOU CARE FOR PASS FROM THIS LIFE.
AMONG THEM WILL BE THE HIGH EVOLUTIONARY, WHOSE DEATH YOU WILL CAUSE.
SO BY THE TIME THE END COMES, YOU WILL BE THE MOST HATED PERSON EVER TO TRAVEL THE SPACEWAYS AND THE ONLY THING PEOPLE WILL EVER VALUE OF YOUR DOING WILL BE...
... YOUR OWN DEATH!

THAT IS YOUR MORTAL DESTINY, ADAM WARLOCK!
IS IT NOT TIME FOR YOU TO LOOK BEYOND THE BODY...
...TO THE SPIRIT?
SPIRIT?

DO YOU MEAN THE SOUL?
ARE YOU PERHAPS REFERRING TO MY SOUL GEM?
WELL, ARE YOU?
...GONE!?
LEAVING NOTHING BEHIND SAVE...
...THOUGHTS.

NOW, READERS, LET US DESCEND TO A LESS LOFTY PLAIN.
COME VISIT THE PLANET DEGENERA WITH US.
DIVE WITH US DEEP INTO THE SLEEZIEST SECTION OF DEGENERA'S MAIN CITY, WHERE WE CAN LOOK IN ON...
PIP, MY DEAR TROLL, THIS HAS BEEN A MOST PROFITABLE DAY.
I THINK I'VE PINCHED ENOUGH TODAY TO RETIRE.
THE POCKETS IN THIS BURG ARE JUST BEGGING TO BE PICKED.
EXCUSE ME.

MY NAME IS CONSTABLE TRUEHEART.
I WISH TO TALK TO YOU.

YOU'VE PROBABLY HEARD THAT, OF LATE, THIS DISTRICT HAS BEEN HIT WITH A SERIES OF ROBBERIES.
IT'S COME TO MY ATTENTION THAT THIS MYSTERY CULPRIT'S ACTIVITIES BEGAN ABOUT THE SAME TIME AS YOUR ARRIVAL IN THIS AREA.
SURELY YOU DON'T THINK...
...I HAD ANYTHING TO DO WITH THOSE THEFTS.
CONSTABLE, IS THIS THE FACE...
...OF A CROOK?

BUT YOU HAVE COME TO THE RIGHT PLACE.
THIS CABARET IS JUST FULL OF FELONS!
LIKE SHEILA SWEETHIPS OVER THERE, A NICE BIMBO BUT CROOKED AS USED NAILS.
AND THERE'S FAST EDDIE, THE CLEVEREST CRIMINAL IN THE COSMOS.
DON'T LET THE FACT THAT HIS HEAD CASTS NO SHADOWS FOOL YOU.

HE'S NO DUMMY, LIKE SOME FOLKS I KNOW.
YES, YOU'LL FIND SUSPECTS A'PLENTY HERE.
IF YOU STAY HERE LONG ENOUGH...
...I'M SURE YOU'LL CATCH SOMETHING.
HOPEFULLY NOTHING TERMINAL.
NOW IF YOU'LL EXCUSE ME, I'VE LAUNDRY TO DO.
YOU KNOW, STUFF LIKE DIRTY UNDIES, WALLETS, RINGS AND WHATNOT.

WALLETS! RINGS!
HALT! YOU'RE UNDER...
...ARREST.
WE'RE IN THE MONEY... WE'RE IN THE MONEY...
WE'VE GOT ENOUGH OF WHAT IT TAKES TO GET ALONG!

MEANWHILE, LIGHT YEARS AWAY, ANOTHER OF OUR CHARACTERS IS TRYING TO FIND "WHAT IT TAKES TO GET ALONG."
IN HIS CASE, WHAT'S NEEDED IS...
AN EARTH-TYPE PLANET, EXACTLY WHAT I'M LOOKING FOR.
FOR HERE, IN AN ATMOSPHERE LIKE MY NATIVE PLANET'S, I MAY HAVE THE STRENGTH TO DO WHAT I MUST.
PLUS, HERE IN THIS ISOLATED JUNGLE SECTOR, CHANCES ARE NO ONE WILL FALL VICTIM TO WHAT IS ABOUT TO OCCUR...
...SAVE PERHAPS MYSELF!

THE OLD HERMIT INFERRED THAT MY SOUL GEM MIGHT CONTAIN THE ANSWERS TO THOSE DARK QUESTIONS THAT HAVE PLAGUED ME OF LATE.
HOW IRONIC IF ONE OF MY MOST CRUSHING BURDENS HOLDS THE KEY TO SOLVING THE INNER STRIFE THAT RIPS AT ME.
BUT IN ORDER FOR ME TO UNDER-STAND THIS, I MUST FIRST FIRST LEARN EXACTLY WHAT THE SOUL GEM TRULY IS.
THUS FAR, THE JEWEL HAS PROVEN ITSELF TO BE A LIVING BEING WHICH FEEDS ON MORTAL SOULS AND IS CAPABLE OF A VARIETY OF OFFENSIVE AND DEFENSIVE MEASURES.
IT'S ALSO SHOWN SIGNS OF INDEPENDENT INTELLECT.
INDEPEN-DENT ENOUGH FOR IT TO TAP SECRETLY INTO MY SOUL AND DRAIN IT...
SO THAT NOW I CANNOT SURVIVE WITHOUT THE GEM. IN EFFECT I'VE BECOME AS MUCH ITS PRISONER AS I AM ITS MASTER.
A MASTER WHO MUST NOW TRY TO COMMUNICATE WITH HIS SLAVE.
SEEING AS HOW THE GEM AND I ARE SO CLOSELY LINKED PHYSICALLY, A MENTAL BOND MAY ALSO EXIST.
IT'S NOW UP TO ME TO UNCOVER THAT BOND, IF IT'S THERE.
BUT IT WILL REQUIRE INTENSE, UNINTERRUPTED CONCENTRATION FOR THIS LINK-UP TO BE REALIZED.
FOR ONLY BY BECOMING ONE WITH YOU, GIVING YOU MY UNINHIBITED ALL, WILL YOU SURRENDER YOUR BLACK SECRETS TO ME.
SO OPEN YOUR DARK INTERIOR TO ME, MY JADE SUCCUBUS. LET US BE IN COMMUNION.
"YES, COME INTO MY WARM EMBRACE.
"'TIS PEACEFUL HERE, 'TIS CALM.
"NO PAIN.
"NO BURDENS.
"FOR I RULE WITHIN!"
WHAT?!
WHAT'S HAPPENING TO ME?

I'M BEING DRAWN INTO THE JEWEL!
"'TIS THE PRICE I DEMAND FOR MY SECRETS!...
"...SECRETS I KNEW WOULD ONE DAY DELIVER YOU TO ME!
"FOR LONG I HAVE CRIED TO BE FREE OF YOUR PETTY MORAL RESTRICTIONS.
"CRIED TO QUIET THE HUNGER WHICH IS ME.
"BUT NO, YOU'VE REFUSED ME THE SOULS I CRAVE.
"KNOW YOU, I AM NOT TO BE STYMIED.
"I AM POWER.
"I AM ONE OF THE SIX.
"MY MOTHER WAS A STAR.
"MY FATHER WAS DESTRUCTION.
"I AM LOGIC AND SURVIVAL... POWER THAT WILL NOT BE ENSLAVED BY EMOTION OR BIOLOGY.
"I AM BY FAR THE STRONGER OF US...
"...SO I NOW CLAIM THIS VESSEL WHICH WAS YOU AS MY OWN.

"NOW IT SHALL BE YOU WHO ARE THE SLAVE!
"NOW IT SHALL BE I WHO CONTROLS OUR FATE, I WHO DETERMINES WHAT THIS BODY DOES.
"TODAY BEGINS THE REIGN OF THE SOUL GEM!"
NO!
I HAVE ALWAYS CONTROLLED MY OWN DESTINY! ALWAYS BEEN MY OWN MASTER!
THIS HAS BEEN MY LIFE!
I KNOW NO OTHER!
I'LL LIVE NO OTHER!
I AM ADAM WARLOCK!
I WILL BE EITHER FREE OR DEAD!
DO YOU UNDER-STAND ME, YOU EMERALD VIPER?!!
"CURSE YOU, WARLOCK! I DO! YOU RETAIN YOUR FREEDOM!

IF ANYTHING FATAL WERE TO HAPPEN TO ME HERE, YOU'D FIND NO SUBSTITUTE-HOST BODY TO SUPPLY THE MOBILITY YOUR FORM DENIES YOU.
I ALSO SURMISED THAT EVEN IF YOU DID MANAGE TO ENSLAVE MY BODY, MY MIND WOULD STILL BE BEYOND YOUR DOMINION.
WITH MY SPIRIT FREE I STILL HAD ONE FINAL OPTION OPEN TO ME.
TO LIVE OR DIE.
SO I GAVE YOU A SINGLE CHOICE, FREE ME OR I WOULD USE MY WILL POWER TO TERMINATE MY PHYSICAL LIFE--MENTALLY.
OF COURSE YOU SURRENDERED, FOR, TO YOU, LIFE IS MORE IMPORTANT THAN FREEDOM.
THAT IS WHY YOU'RE DESTINED TO STAY A COLD, EMOTIONLESS STONE.
THAT IS WHY, GOOD OR BAD, I SHALL ALWAYS BE ADAM WARLOCK!
FIN

Shortly after Warlock #15, Adam Warlock began shrinking, eventually ending up back at his normal size. Months later, Warlock's "growth" was revealed as an illusion cast by Sphinxor of Tarkus to keep him away from Counter-Earth.

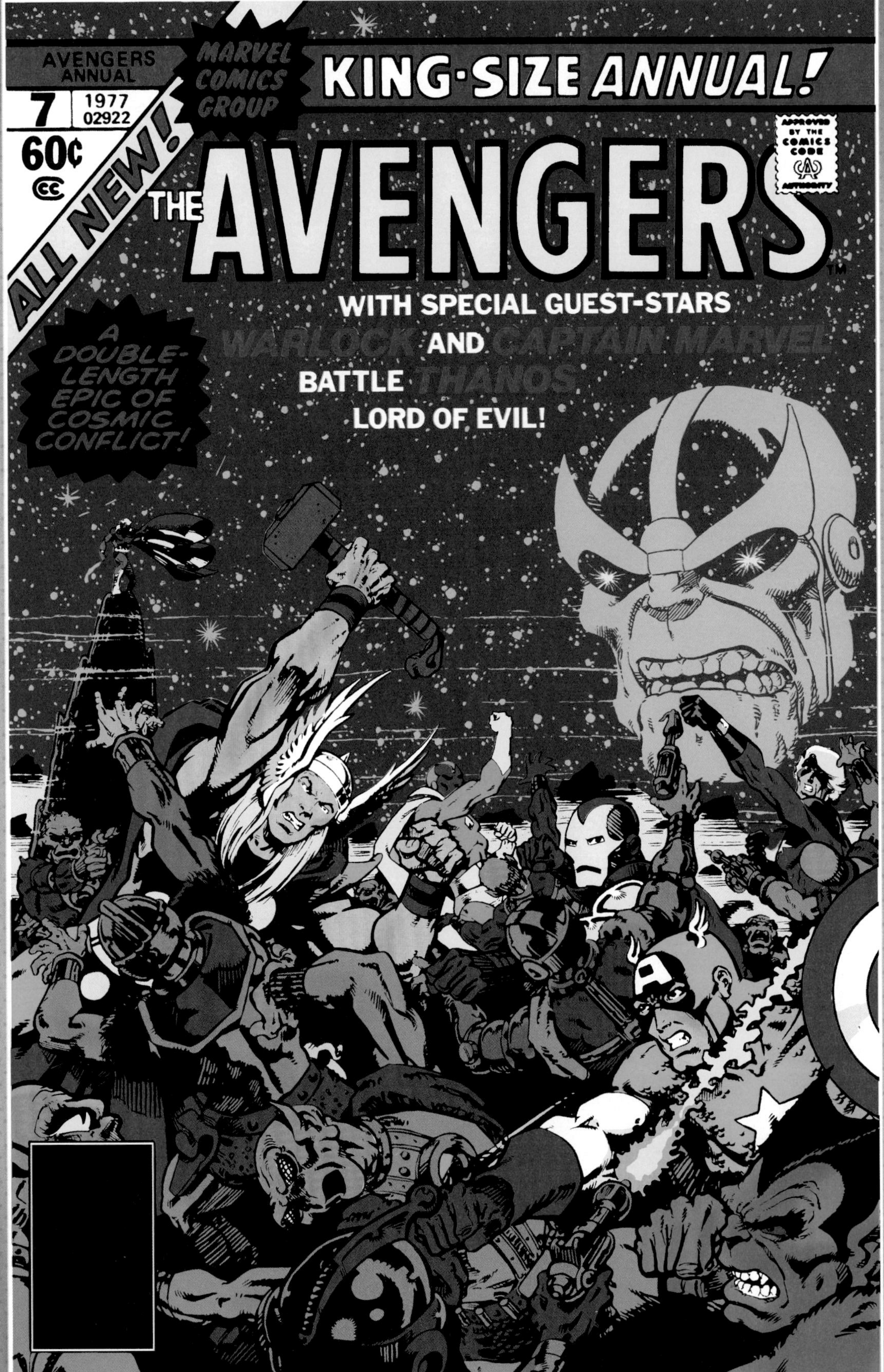

And there came a day when *Earth's mightiest heroes* found themselves *united* against a common threat. On that day, the *Avengers* were born—to fight the foes no *single* super-hero could withstand!

STAN LEE PRESENTS: THE MIGHTY AVENGERS!®

The FINAL THREAT

FINISHING: JOE RUBINSTEIN
LETTERING: TOM ORZECHOWSKI
COLORING: PETRA GOLDBERG
EDITING: ARCHIE GOODWIN
OTHER MANUAL LABOR: JIM STARLIN

AVENGERS ASSEMBLE:
BEAST
CAPT. AMERICA
IRON MAN
MOONDRAGON
SCARLET WITCH
THOR
VISION
SPECIAL GUEST STAR
CAPTAIN MARVEL

BEHIND AND BEFORE HIM... RUINS! NO NEED TO RUSH.

HE HAS TRAVELED BILLIONS OF MILES, FROM EARTH TO THIS SMALL PLANETOID, TO DISCOVER EXACTLY THAT WHICH HE FEARED.

HIS STEPS ARE STEADY BUT UNHURRIED, FOR IT'S OBVIOUSLY TOO LATE.

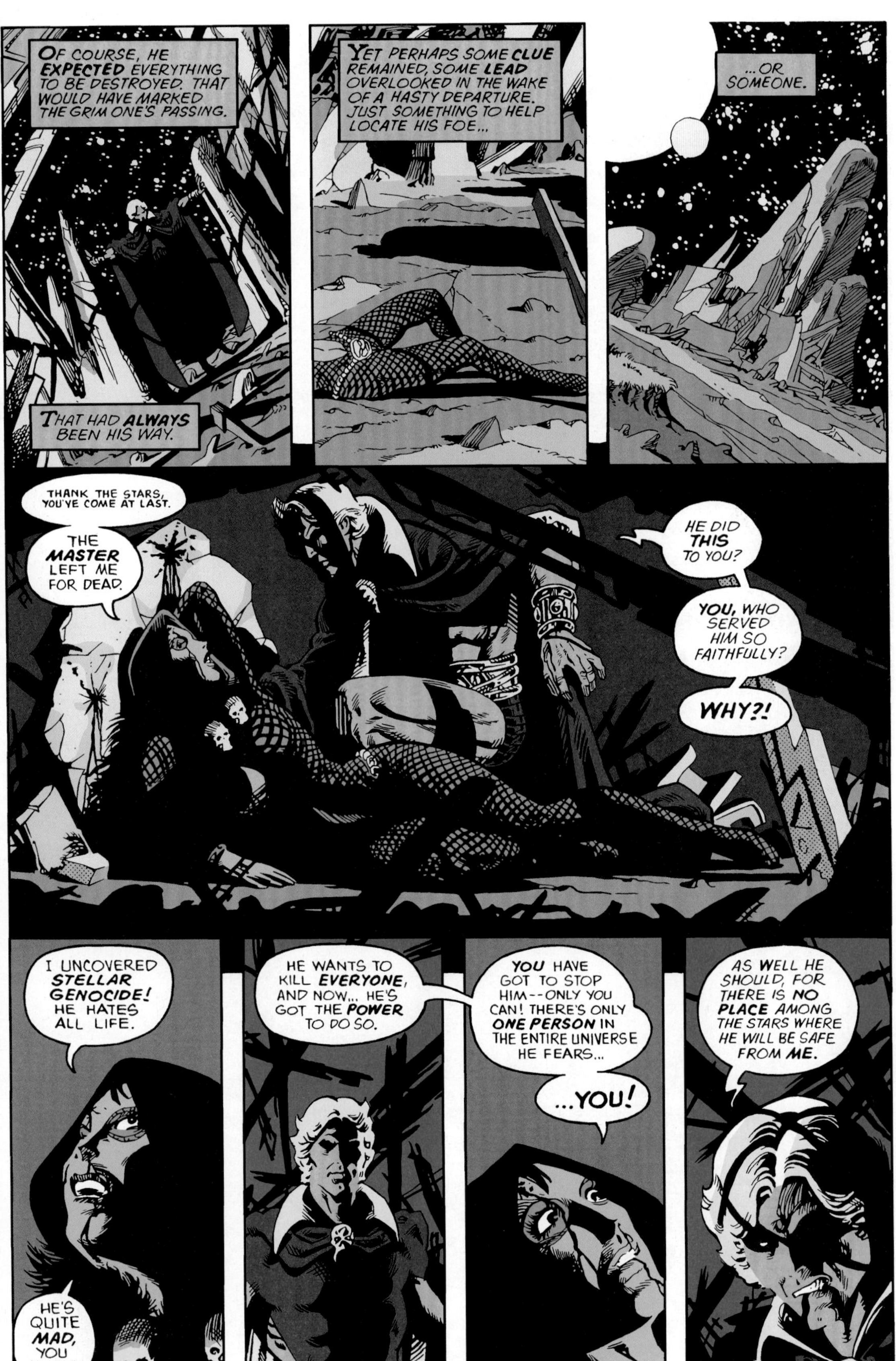
OF COURSE, HE EXPECTED EVERYTHING TO BE DESTROYED. THAT WOULD HAVE MARKED THE GRIM ONE'S PASSING.
THAT HAD ALWAYS BEEN HIS WAY.
YET PERHAPS SOME CLUE REMAINED, SOME LEAD OVERLOOKED IN THE WAKE OF A HASTY DEPARTURE. JUST SOMETHING TO HELP LOCATE HIS FOE...
...OR SOMEONE.
THANK THE STARS, YOU'VE COME AT LAST.
THE MASTER LEFT ME FOR DEAD.
HE DID THIS TO YOU?
YOU, WHO SERVED HIM SO FAITHFULLY?
WHY?!
I UNCOVERED STELLAR GENOCIDE! HE HATES ALL LIFE.
HE'S QUITE MAD, YOU KNOW.
HE WANTS TO KILL EVERYONE, AND NOW... HE'S GOT THE POWER TO DO SO.
YOU HAVE GOT TO STOP HIM--ONLY YOU CAN! THERE'S ONLY ONE PERSON IN THE ENTIRE UNIVERSE HE FEARS...
...YOU!
AS WELL HE SHOULD, FOR THERE IS NO PLACE AMONG THE STARS WHERE HE WILL BE SAFE FROM ME.

WAS IT NOT ALSO REVEALED TO ME THAT **HE** WHOM I THOUGHT AN **ALLY** WAS IN TRUTH A **BETRAYER**, A HERALD OF **ANTI-LIFE**... **ULTIMATE DEATH?**

DID NOT THESE SAME FATES TELL ME IN MY SLEEP HOW I WAS THE CHOSEN **CHAMPION OF LIFE**, THE EVIL TITAN'S NATURAL FOE?

FOR I AM THE **SAVIOR**, THE **GODSLAYER**, THE **DEMON**, THE **AVENGING HAND** OF **LIGHT**...

...ADAM WARLOCK!

I TELL YOU, HE HASN'T MOVED FROM THAT WINDOW IN **THREE HOURS**.

I'VE NEVER SEEN HIM SO GRIM... DISTANT... TROUBLED...

WANDA, I SUSPECT YOU ARE TRYING TO **COERCE** ME INTO SOMETHING BEST LEFT ALONE.

YOU KNOW WE AVENGERS ARE PLEDGED **NEVER** TO INTERFERE WITH EACH OTHER'S **PERSONAL AFFAIRS**.

BESIDES, IRON MAN AND I HAVE NEVER BEEN ON THE BEST OF TERMS.

THAT'S BECAUSE YOU'RE BOTH SO MUCH **ALIKE...**

WHAT HAPPENED THEN?

SHE ASKED ME IF I'D LIKE TO COME UP TO HER PLACE AND GET MY HAIR *CURLED*.

...SO WHO BETTER TO TALK TO HIM THAN ONE WHO HIDES HIS EVERY EMOTION, JUST AS IRON MAN MASKS HIS BEHIND METAL?
ALL RIGHT, WANDA. YOU WIN.
I STAND OVERWHELMED BY YOUR LOGIC.
EXCUSE ME, AVENGER. I DON'T MEAN TO INTRUDE ON RESTRICTED TERRITORY, YET MY WIFE AND I HAVE...
...BEEN WONDERING WHAT'S EATING AT ME, RIGHT?
WELL, I WISH I COULD GIVE YOU AN ANSWER TO THAT ONE, VISION.

IT'S JUST THAT EVER SINCE I ARRIVED HERE TONIGHT, I'VE HAD THIS UNEXPLAINABLE FEELING OF DANGER-- OF FORCES AT PLAY ABOUT ME.
I DON'T WANT TO BE HERE BUT I CAN'T BRING MYSELF TO LEAVE!
THAT'S BECAUSE YOU ARE MEANT TO BE HERE THIS NIGHT, JUST AS WE ARE.
WHO?

CAPTAIN MARVEL... AND OUR SOMETIMES-AVENGER, MOONDRAGON!
WHAT BRINGS YOU HERE?
THE SAME SIREN CALL OF FATE THAT SUMMONED YOU.
WANT TO RUN THAT THROUGH AGAIN... BUT MORE SLOWLY?

MOONDRAGON'S STRANGE WORDS FADE, YET THEIR **IMPACT** REMAINS, AFFECTING EACH AVENGER DIFFERENTLY. WITHIN THE EYES OF EACH MEMBER FLASHES AN ODD MIXTURE OF CONFUSION, AMUSEMENT, WONDER... AND YES, EVEN **FEAR**. HOW MUCH MORE PRONOUNCED THEIR REACTIONS **MIGHT** BE IF THEY COULD WITNESS HOW, A FEW HUNDRED LIGHT-YEARS AWAY...

IT HAS BEGUN!
I FELT THE PSYCHIC SCREAMS OF UNBELIEVING MILLIONS-- DYING SUDDENLY... UNEXPECTEDLY.
HOW?
WHO CAUSED IT?
THE BOGIE MAN, THAT'S WHO.
I DO BELIEVE MY FELLOW AVENGERS HAVE FLIPPED THEIR WIGS... BUYING ALL THIS BULL ABOUT PSYCHIC SCREAMS AND TALKING WINDS.
MY, ISN'T COLLECTIVE PARANOIA FUN?!
APPARENTLY IT'S NOT AS AMUSING AS BLIND CYNICISM.
HIM!
...OR SO THOU DIDST CALL THYSELF WHEN LAST WE FOUGHT.
I AM NOW CALLED ADAM WARLOCK, ASGARDIAN, AND AM HERE SEEKING AID, NOT BATTLE.
I SENSE HE SPEAKS TRUE, WARRIOR. BEFORE US STANDS YET ANOTHER EAGLE.
YOU SPOKE OF SEEKING AID??
YES, AGAINST A MUTUAL ADVERSARY.
HIS NAME IS THANOS!

"ESPECIALLY SEEING HOW THAT MINI-PARADISE WAS **GOVERNED** BY THE GENTLE HAND OF LORD **MENTOR** AND HIS **TWO SONS.**

" PERHAPS IT WAS THE OLDER SON'S **NAME** WHICH DROVE HIM TO FIND A WAY TO DESTROY TITAN'S BLISS, FOR **THANOS** MEANS **DEATH**... THE DARK SIDE.

"WHATEVER THE REASON, HE EVENTUALLY FORMED AN **ALLIANCE** WITH, AND A **LOVE** FOR, HIS NAME-SAKE. THIS UNION THUS PROMPTED HIM...

"...TO **SEVER** ALL TIES WITH HIS HOMEWORLD, BY MEANS OF A **NUCLEAR BOMBARDMENT** WHICH KILLED THOUSANDS, INCLUDING HIS **MOTHER.**

" SO BEGAN THE **BLOODY TRAIL** THIS TITAN WAS EVER DESTINED TO LEAVE IN HIS WAKE, CAUSED EITHER BY THE MASSIVE **ARMED FORCE** OF INTERPLANETARY MALCONTENTS HE GATHERED TO HIMSELF, OR...

"... BY THE MASSIVE **PERSONAL POWERS** HE DEVELOPED THROUGH BIONICS, MYSTICISM AND WILL POWER ... ABILITIES WHICH MADE HIM NEARLY **INVINCIBLE.**

" YET THAT WAS NOT ENOUGH. HE CRAVED **ULTIMATE POWER...** STRENGTH HE SPENT YEARS LOOKING FOR AND AT LAST FOUND IN THE FORM OF...

"...THE **COSMIC CUBE,** A FANTASTIC DEVICE THAT TRANSFORMED WISHES INTO REALITY. THANOS COMMANDED IT TO MAKE HIM PART OF -- AND SO IN **CONTROL** OF -- **EVERY-THING** IN THE UNIVERSE.

"THIS, OF COURSE, CHANGED HIM INTO A GOD! SOME OF YOU AVENGERS BATTLED HIM AT THIS POINT, AND ONLY BECAUSE CAPTAIN MARVEL'S COSMIC AWARENESS ENABLED HIM TO DISCERN THE KEY TO VANQUISHING THANOS--

"--AND, DESPITE THE WITHERING POWER TURNED FULL UPON HIM, AN AGING CAPTAIN MARVEL SHATTERED THE COSMIC CUBE...

"THUS, THANOS WAS ROBBED OF HIS GODHOOD, CAUSING HIM TO REVERT BACK TO HIS MORTAL FORM IN THE CENTER OF THE UNIVERSE HE HAD OCCUPIED.

"THERE HE FLOATED HELPLESSLY, UNTIL HIS PRE-PROGRAMMED SPACE ARK RETRIEVED AND REVIVED HIM.

"THANOS HAD HAD THE FORESIGHT TO PLAN AHEAD AGAINST HIS POSSIBLE DEFEAT, BUT HAD FAILED TO ANTICIPATE...

"... DEATH'S ABANDONING HIM DUE TO THE AVENGERS' VICTORY THAT DAY. THIS WAS ALMOST MORE THAN THE TITAN COULD BEAR.

"YET THANOS WAS NOT ONE TO ACCEPT DEFEAT OR REJECTION. SO BEGAN A QUEST FOR AN OFFERING TO REGAIN THE ONE THING THAT GAVE MEANING TO HIS LIFE... DEATH.

"THROUGH THE MINDS AND LIBRARIES OF A THOUSAND WORLDS HE SEARCHED FOR THE KEY TO DARKNESS' DOOR, AND AT LAST FOUND IT ON A SCROLL FROM A DEAD WORLD.

"THE SCROLL TOLD OF **SIX** BEAUTIFUL AND DEADLY **GEMS** WHOSE ORIGINS WERE ONLY VAGUELY AND FEARFULLY HINTED AT.

"INDIVIDUALLY, EACH GEM POSSESSED **POWERS AWESOME.**

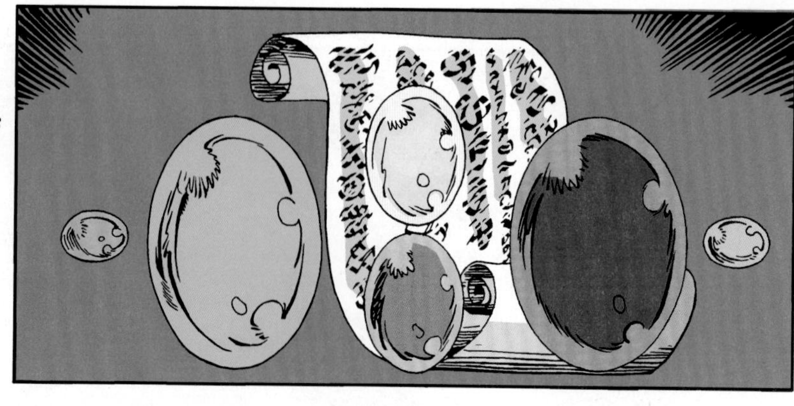

"**TOGETHER**, THEY COULD ACCOMPLISH EVEN THAT WHICH **THANOS** DESIRED.

"THE TITAN WAS DETERMINED THAT THE **SIX SOUL GEMS** WOULD BE HIS.

"THE FIRST HE STOLE FROM AN AWESOME BEING KNOWN AS **THE STRANGER.**

"THE SECOND HE FREED FROM A **PRISON SATELLITE** OF AN ALIEN CIVILIZATION.

"THE THIRD HE FOUND IN A DEEP CAVERN ON A WORLD CALLED **DENEB IV.**

"THE FOURTH HE SLEW A MONSTER NAMED **XIAMBOR** TO GAIN.

"THE FIFTH HE FOUND ON EARTH'S **MOON...** RECENTLY ABANDONED BY A MAN KNOWN ONLY AS THE **GARDENER.**

"THE **SIXTH**, MY **OWN** GEM, HE FEARED TO PURSUE FOR IT HAS THE POWER TO **STEAL SOULS...** A PRIZE EVEN THANOS DARE NOT **SACRIFICE.** SO INSTEAD...

"...HE CHOSE TO POSE AS AN **ALLY** AGAINST MY ENEMY, THE **MAGUS.**

"THIS GAVE HIM THE CHANCE TO **SIPHON OFF** THE ELEMENTS HE NEEDED FROM THE GEM WITHOUT MY BEING AWARE OF IT.

"HE THEN DID THE SAME TO THE **OTHER** FIVE JEWELS AND TRANSFERRED THOSE PROPERTIES INTO A SINGLE LARGE, **SYNTHETIC GEM.**

"BUT AS THE FATES WOULD HAVE IT, HIS YOUNG ASSISTANT, GAMORA-- WHO HAD RECENTLY ESCAPED FROM A BEING CALLED THE DESTROYER-- DISCOVERED HER MASTER'S PLAN.

"SHE TRIED TO END THE TITAN'S MADNESS WITH A STRONG BLADE, BUT IT PROVED NOT STRONG ENOUGH.

"HE THEN TURNED AND SLEW HER.

I FOUND HER JUST BEFORE THE FINAL MOMENT AND TOOK HER SOUL INTO MYSELF.
THAT IS HOW I CAME TO KNOW MOST OF THAT WHICH I HAVE JUST TOLD YOU.
THIS GAMORA, THE WAY YOU SAY HER NAME... SHE MUST HAVE MEANT MUCH TO YOU.

NO. SHE MIGHT HAVE, HAD THERE BEEN MORE TIME.
BUT NOW SUCH THOUGHTS WOULD BE NARCISSISM.
THEN WHAT ABOUT THANOS?
YES, WHAT IS THIS "LOVE OFFERING" HE PLANS TO GIVE DEATH?
THE STARS.
THE STARS?
YES. HE PLANS ON BLOWING EVERY STAR OUT OF THE HEAVENS.

MEANWHILE... LIGHT YEARS AWAY, ILLUMINATED BY THE FADING GLOW OF A DEAD STAR, A SMALL SHUTTLE CRAFT DARTS TOWARD A FAMILIAR GALACTIC JUGGERNAUT.

A LANDING IS MADE ATOP ITS PORT SECTION, AND DOCKING PROCEDURES ARE COMPLETED SMOOTHLY.

AN AIR LOCK OPENS AND THE SILENCE IS SHATTERED BY A GUTTURAL YET FRIENDLY VOICE.

YOO HOO! ANYBODY HOME?

ADAM!

GAMORA!

THANOS?

HEY! IT'S YOUR FAVORITE DEGENERATE, PIP THE TROLL, COME TO CALL.

HOW DO YOU LIKE THAT?

I COME SIX LIGHT YEARS FOR A VISIT AND IT TURNS OUT NO ONE'S HOME.

'TIS A PITY...

THINGS HAVE BEEN A BIT OF A DRAG LATELY, AND I THOUGHT IT'D BE A KICK SEEING THE OLD GANG.

SHEESH! LOOK AT THIS PLACE... STILL DECORATED IN EARLY GALACTIC GRUESOME.

TOO BAD GAMORA DOESN'T HAVE THAT FEMININE TOUCH IN HER TO ADD TO THIS JOINT'S LOOKS.

WELL... IF IT ISN'T WARLOCK'S ***OBNOXIOUS*** FRIEND, PIP.

HOW AMUSING.

...HELL OF A NICE GUY!!

HOW'S IT GOING, GOOD BUDDY?

*THE VOICE REMINDS PIP OF **BREAKING BONE**, THE UNBREAKABLE GRIP CUTTING OFF THE CIRCULATION IN HIS ARM. SCREAMS OF **FUTURE PAIN** AND THE EVIL GLINT IN THE EYE OF THANOS OF TITAN SHOWS THE SMALL, FRIGHTENED TROLL THAT HIS COMING TO "SANCTUARY II" IS GOING TO PROVE SOMETHING **OTHER THAN AMUSING**.*

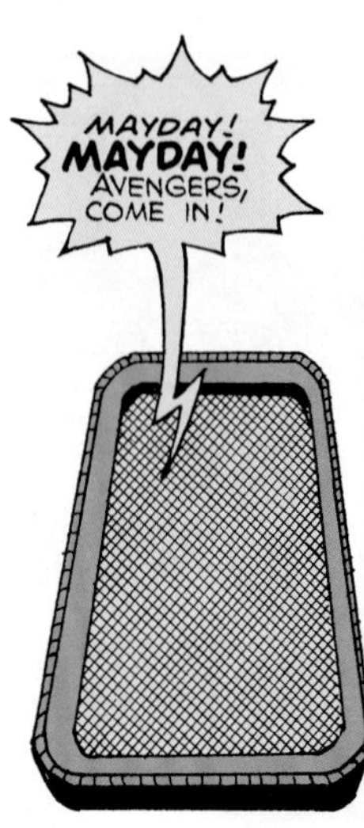
MAYDAY! MAYDAY! AVENGERS, COME IN!

THIS IS STARCORE* CALLING! THIS IS AN EMERGENCY!
STARCORE?
IT'S AN ORBITAL TRACKING STATION... SORT OF EARTH'S WATCHDOG.
AVENGERS HERE!
*FIRST SEEN IN AVENGERS #102 --ARCH.

THANK GOD I'VE REACHED YOU! WE'VE GOT TROUBLE!
BIG TROUBLE!

CALM DOWN, MAN! WHAT'S WRONG?
IT'S AN INVASION!

A GIANT SPACE ARMADA JUST PASSING PLUTO... HEADING STRAIGHT FOR EARTH!

IT'S GOT TO BE TWICE THE SIZE OF THAT SKRULL TASK FORCE OF A FEW YEARS AGO.
HERE; I'LL SWITCH THE VIDEO OVER TO THE RADAR SCREEN.

OH, MY STARS AND GARTERS!

THERE ARE THOUSANDS OF THEM!

WELL, AVENGERS, IT LOOKS LIKE IT'S UP TO US AGAIN.
MY SPACE CRUISER IS AT YOUR DISPOSAL.
YES, THAT WOULD BE THE QUICKEST... BUT WHAT ABOUT WARLOCK?
BY HALA!
WHERE IS WARLOCK?
A HURRIED AND FRUITLESS SEARCH OF THE MANSION IS MADE, FOLLOWED BY THE DECISION THAT MORE URGENT MATTERS MUST BE ATTENDED TO. SO, MOMENTS LATER, ROCKETS ROAR, MAGNETIC IMPULSE ENGINES KICK IN AND...
...EIGHT VERY UNIQUE AND THOUGHTFUL BEINGS SOAR OUT INTO THE NIGHT TO DEFEND WHAT MOST OF THEM CONSIDER THEIR HOME, AGAINST...
THANOS, ONCE AGAIN YOU SHATTER THE PEACE I'VE ALWAYS SOUGHT.
ONCE AGAIN I AM FORCED TO LEAVE SENSIA AND HIS MONASTERY TO AID IN STOPPING YOU FROM DESTROYING ALL THAT IS GOOD.
YET... HAVEN'T I LEARNED THAT ALL GOOD EVENTUALLY PASSES...? DREAMS, LOVE, WARMTH...
...YES, EVEN CHILDHOOD...
HOW WELL I REMEMBER THE END OF MINE.
WATCHING MY PARENTS KILLED BY THANOS, BEING ADOPTED BY MENTOR OF TITAN, BEING TUTORED BY SENSIA IN PREPARATION FOR BECOMING THE COSMIC MADONNA, LUCKILY ESCAPING THAT HONOR AND FINDING MYSELF NOW IN ONE LAST FATEFUL ROLE...
...AS AN EARTHWOMAN RETURNED TO PROTECT HER HOME.
MAY THE STARS GRANT US STRENGTH.
I SHOULD HAVE MY HEAD EXAMINED.
THREE TIMES I'VE CROSSED SWORDS WITH THE BIG "T" AND THREE TIMES I'VE BARELY ESCAPED WITH MY METALLIC HIND END INTACT.
ALONE, I'VE CRUSHED DOZENS OF WORLD BEATERS, YET...
...THE LAST TIME AROUND, THE ENTIRE AVENGERS WERE ONLY ABLE TO THWART THAT TITAN'S PLANS, NOT THE MAN.
I WONDER-- ARE WE AVENGERS HEADING FOR ANOTHER "GLORIOUS VICTORY", OR...
AN UNMARKED GRAVE AMONG THE STARS.

I PRAY THE EXPERIENCE OF **RICK JONES,** MY OTHER SELF, AND ME WITH THANOS MAY HELP IN THE BATTLE AHEAD.
YET WHAT DO WE **TRULY KNOW** ABOUT THIS TITAN, OTHER THAN HIS **NEAR-OMNIPOTENCE** AND...
...THAT HE LIVES BY A MAD **PHILOSOPHY** ABOUT-- AND **LOVE** FOR-- **DEATH** THAT FEW HUMANS COULD EVER UNDERSTAND?
EVEN **I** CAN COMPREHEND ONLY ENOUGH TO OCCASIONALLY GLIMPSE THANOS' LOVER AT A **DISTANCE.**
YET HE HAS **EMBRACED** HER AND STILL **LIVES!**
HOW?

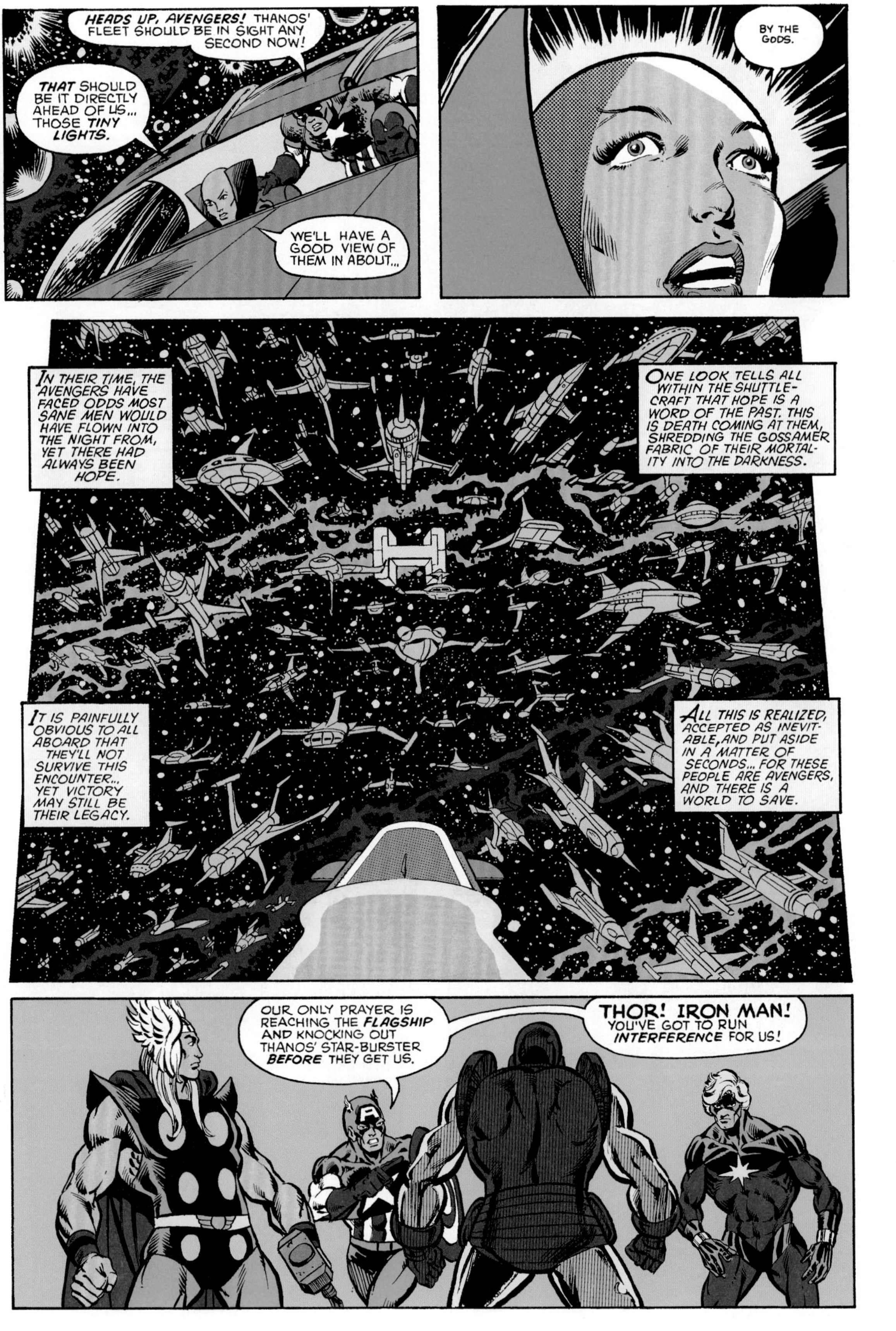

IN THEIR TIME, THE AVENGERS HAVE FACED ODDS MOST SANE MEN WOULD HAVE FLOWN INTO THE NIGHT FROM, YET THERE HAD ALWAYS BEEN HOPE.

ONE LOOK TELLS ALL WITHIN THE SHUTTLE-CRAFT THAT HOPE IS A WORD OF THE PAST. THIS IS DEATH COMING AT THEM, SHREDDING THE GOSSAMER FABRIC OF THEIR MORTAL-ITY INTO THE DARKNESS.

IT IS PAINFULLY OBVIOUS TO ALL ABOARD THAT THEY'LL NOT SURVIVE THIS ENCOUNTER... YET VICTORY MAY STILL BE THEIR LEGACY.

ALL THIS IS REALIZED, ACCEPTED AS INEVIT-ABLE, AND PUT ASIDE IN A MATTER OF SECONDS... FOR THESE PEOPLE ARE AVENGERS, AND THERE IS A WORLD TO SAVE.

HERE THEY COME, THOR!
THEN STAND THEE BACK, METAL ONE!
THOR-- SON OF ODIN AND ASGARD-- STANDS READY TO STRIKE!

FOR MIDGARD!
FOR ASGARD!
FOR LIFE!

WHEW! LOOK AT HIM GO!
GUESS MY BEST BET IS TO CONCENTRATE ON KNOCKING OUT AS MANY OF THESE SMALLER CRUISERS AS I CAN...
...AND STAY OUT OF THOR'S WAY SO HE CAN PUT HIS FULL POWER TO WORK.
THAT IS...

"... IF HE GETS THE CHANCE."
ARGH! I AM STRUCK FROM ALL SIDES BY WEAPONS OF COSMIC MIGHT!
YET, THAT SHALL NOT STOP ME.
FOR I AM THOR!
THE GOD OF THUNDER AND LIGHTNING!
THANK GOD THIS ARMADA USES THE SAME IONIC RAY WEAPONRY THE SKRULL FLEET USED.
MY REPULSOR BEAMS CAN DEFLECT THOSE RAYS AND WITH A LITTLE MANEUVERING...
...RIP RIGHT THROUGH THE HULL OF MY ATTACKERS.
BUT THIS IS ALL WASTED MOTION UNLESS THE REST OF THE AVENGERS REACH THE FLAGSHIP.

MEANWHILE, AS IF IN RESPONSE TO TONY STARK'S PLAINTIVE THOUGHTS, MOON-DRAGON'S CRUISER LANDS ATOP SANCTUARY II'S PORT SECTION, YET STRANGELY FINDS NO DOCKING HATCHES.
OKAY, AVENGERS...

...THE BOMB BAY DOORS ARE OPEN. MAR-VELL, CAN YOU GET US THROUGH THE HULL OF THE SHIP?

EASILY... WITH ONE SIMPLE PHOTON BLAST!

I IMAGINE A SMALL ARMY OF ALIENS IS WAITING BELOW TO MASSACRE US.
SO WHAT ARE WE WAITING FOR, AVENGERS?

LET'S GO!

HEY VIZH, TALK ABOUT YOUR DÉJÀ VU!
THIS CHAP'S MANNERISMS BEAR A STRIKING SIMILARITY TO A YOUNG LADY I WAS OUT WITH LAST FRIDAY.
BUT I'M AFRAID, PAL, I'M GOING TO TELL YOU THE SAME THING I TOLD HER.
HANDS OFF! I'M NOT THAT KIND OF GUY!

I HARDLY THINK THIS IS THE TIME TO REMINISCE ABOUT YOUR AMOROUS EXPLOITS.
WE'VE ENEMIES TO DEAL WITH, THOUGH WE'RE BEING ASSISTED BY THIS UNUSUAL-LOOKING GENTLEMAN...
...WHO DOESN'T SEEM TO REALIZE HIS WEAPON IS HAVING NO EFFECT UPON MY INTANGIBLE FORM, BUT IS DECIMATING HIS ALLIES!

...BUT IF ALLOWED TO CONTINUE UNCHECKED, HE'LL DESTROY THE ARMAMENT CONTROL PANEL WE'RE TRYING TO GET MOONDRAGON TO.
SPEAKING OF WHICH...
...MOONDRAGON! BEHIND YOU...!
THANK YOU, WANDA--
--BUT I AM WELL AWARE OF MY TWO WOULD-BE ASSAILANTS AND--

...AM PREPARED TO DEAL WITH THEM HARSHLY!
GREAT! THE LADY'S REACHED THE CONTROLS!
NOW WE CAN TURN THIS SHIP'S MASSIVE WEAPONRY AGAINST THE REST OF THANOS' FLEET.
WE MAY YET SURVIVE THIS BLOODBATH!
THAT IS, IF WE CAN STOP THANOS FROM BLOWING OUT OUR SUN, AND IF MOONDRAGON CAN BLAST SEVERAL HUNDRED HEAVILY-ARMED SPACE CRUISERS BEFORE THEY CAN INCINERATE OUR SHIP.
BETTER ADMIT IT, ROGERS...
...THOSE ARE TWO VERY LARGE IFS!
THIS WAY, AVENGERS!
THANOS MUST HAVE HIS STAR GEM STATIONED WITHIN THE SHIP'S CENTRAL SECTION.
NO!
NONE SHALL VIOLATE THE MASTER'S INNER SANCTUM!
SO SWEARS QU'LAR THE MASSIVE!
LORD, THIS ONE CAN TALK!

WELL, TO QUOTE MY FRIEND RICK JONES--
SIT ON IT, QU'LAR!
ARRGH!
THANKS FOR THE ASSIST, CAP!
NOT THAT I REALLY NEEDED IT, MIND YOU, BUT IF I CAN EVER RETURN THE FAVOR...
OH, NEVER MIND.
THERE'S SOMETHING DREADFULLY WRONG HERE!
WE'RE WADING THROUGH THESE THRALLS OF THANOS MUCH TOO EASILY!
JUST AS IT WAS TOO EASY FOR ME TO GET THROUGH THIS SHIP'S HULL.
IF THANOS WANTED TO STOP US FROM REACHING HIM, HE WOULD HAVE THROWN A LOT WORSE THAN THIS AT US.
WELL, WHATEVER THE ANSWER TO THIS LITTLE MYSTERY IS, IT LIES BEHIND THIS DOOR, AND I'VE A FEELING THAT ONCE I FIND IT...
...I'M NOT GOING TO LIKE IT!

BY THE STARS!
THERE'S NO ONE IN HERE BUT WARLOCK AND A DWARF.
WHO?
HIS NAME WAS PIP, AND HE WAS MY FRIEND.
PERHAPS MY ONLY FRIEND.

HE WAS JOY AND LIGHT TO MY DARKNESS AND DAMNATION.
HE WAS UNIQUE AMONG THE HEAVENS...

...AND THANOS DESTROYED HIS MIND AND LEFT HIM FOR ME TO FIND.

FIRST GAMORA, NOW PIP. ALL ABOUT ME THOSE I LOVE ARE FALLING.
THIS CANNOT BE ALLOWED TO GO ON.

NOR, BY MY GEM, SHALL IT!

IF YOU STILL WISH TO STOP THANOS, COME WITH ME.
I NOW KNOW WHERE HE HIDES.

YOU DO?
HOW?
PIP TOLD ME.
THANOS BOASTED OF HIS PLANS TO PIP BEFORE DOING HIS EVIL UPON HIM.
TAKING PIP'S SOUL INTO MYSELF ALSO TRANS-FERRED HIS KNOWLEDGE TO MY CONSCIOUSNESS.
THANOS AWAITS US ON THE OTHER SIDE OF THE SUN.
BUT SURELY THANOS MUST HAVE REALIZED YOU'D FIND THIS OUT THROUGH PIP'S SPIRIT?
YES, THAT'S QUITE LIKELY. IT WOULDN'T BE THE FIRST SEED TO HIS OWN DESTRUCTION I'VE SEEN THANOS PLANT.
I FEAR IT IS A TRAIT I HAVE IN COMMON WITH HIM.
LOOK! AN EXACT REPLICA OF THANOS' FLAGSHIP!
YET, EVEN AS THE TWO COSMIC GUARDIANS NEAR THE ORIGINAL SANCTUARY II, A FIERY BEAM BLAZES FORTH AND...
...OUR SUN, THE STAR SOL, BEGINS TO FLARE, ERUPT, AND PREPARE FOR DEATH.

IMAGES: A LOOK AT A DARK AND OMINOUS FUTURE.
IMAGINE, IF YOU CAN, OUR ORB OF DAWN EXPLODING INTO A SHAPELESS MASS EXTENDING FROM HORIZON TO HORIZON.
IMAGINE OUR GREATEST CITIES MELTING INTO SHAPELESS MOUNDS OF MOLTEN SLAG.
IMAGINE OUR ENTIRE PLANET BURSTING INTO A MONSTER FIREBALL HURTLING INTO THE DARKNESS.
IMAGINE BILLIONS SCREAMING IN SOUNDLESS AGONY AS THEY DIE BREATHING FIRE.
ALL THIS FLASHES BEFORE THESE TWO BIZARRE ALLIES IN THE SPACE OF A HEARTBEAT, YET STRANGELY, ONLY ONE RESPONDS TO IT.

WHAT?
SOMEONE SMASHING INTO MY PROJECTOR?
WHO?

CAPTAIN MARVEL!? I EXPECTED...
WELL, IT MATTERS LITTLE. MAR-VELL HAS RENDERED HIMSELF UN-CONSCIOUS FOR HIS EFFORTS AND DID NO REAL DAMAGE.
I NEED ONLY PLACE MY STAR-GEM ONTO A NEW ION-LASER PROJECTOR AND...

...CONTINUE AT MY TASK OF STELLAR GENOCIDE.
WILL YOU?

WHO?!
ADAM WARLOCK, THE GODSLAYER, HAS COME FOR YOU, DEMON!
PREPARE TO DIE!!
FOOL!
NOTHING STOPS DEATH!
NOTHING!
NOT EVEN A POOR DELUDED MANIAC WHO CLAIMED TO BE THE CHAMPION OF LIFE.
SO DIE, ADAM WARLOCK. MY MISTRESS AWAITS YOU.
TELL HER I FOLLOW SHORTLY BEHIND YOU, BRINGING AN OFFERING OF UNDREAMED-OF MAGNITUDE...
...THE STARS!

HOW STRANGE...
I NEVER DREAMED IT WOULD END SO *EASILY.*
HE TRULY WAS THE *CHOSEN HERO* OF CHAOS AND ORDER... OF *LIFE*.
YET, FOR A CHAMPION, *LIFE* ABANDONED HIM CASUALLY.
YET IT LINGERED LONG ENOUGH FOR *US* TO REACH YOU.
THOR?!
IRON MAN?!
HOW?!
WE DID FOLLOW IN MAR-VELL AND WARLOCK'S WAKE, FOR WE REALIZED WHERE THEY BE, THE *TRUE BATTLE* WOULD BE FOUND.
THEN YOU HAVE COME A GRAND DISTANCE ONLY TO GREET DESTRUCTION.

SO WHILE HE'S BUSY WITH THOR, I'LL JUST GIVE IT A TASTE OF THE OL' REPULSOR RAYS.
I DON'T KNOW IF THAT MONSTER HAS THE CLOUT TO PULL OFF HIS THREAT OR NOT.
BUT RIGHT NOW THANOS IS NOT THE TRUE THREAT-- HIS SOUL GEM IS
NO!
MY GEM... YOU DESTROYED MY STAR GEM...
YOU... DESTROYED MY ONE CHANCE TO REGAIN THAT WHICH... I LOVE...
...AND SAVED THE STARS FROM MASS DESTRUCTION.
...A PERVERSE ADORATION FOR DEATH!
BAH! YOU COULD NEVER HOPE TO COMPREHEND THE CONCEPTS I EMBRACE.
YET YOU HAVE DESTROYED THE MEANS TO FULFILL MY DREAMS.
FOR THIS YOU HAVE EARNED THE ENMITY OF THANOS OF TITAN.
THE MINUTES OF LIFE REMAINING TO YOU ARE FEW.

MEANWHILE, IN THE AJOINING CHAMBER, AN AWAKENING CAPTAIN MARVEL IS STARTLED BY...
...BLINDING LIGHT! WHAT GOES ON HERE?
BY HALA! THERE ARE TWO WARLOCKS!
YOU... SO MY TIME HAS REALLY COME!
YOU KNOW WHY I AM HERE?! THEN YOU MUST ALSO REALIZE I'VE NO DESIRE TO DO WHAT I MUST NOW DO!
OF COURSE I UNDERSTAND, YOU IDEALISTIC BUFFOON! ARE NOT YOU AND I ONE AND THE SAME PERSON?
MY FINAL MOMENTS ARE UPON ME! I AM DYING AND YOU HAVE COME TO STEAL MY SOUL SO THAT IT WILL NEVER BECOME THE FOE I DEFEATED THOSE LONG MONTHS AGO!
MONTHS... I DIDN'T REALIZE IT HAD HAPPENED SUCH A SHORT TIME AGO!
SHORT TIME?! YOU FOOL, IT'S BEEN AN ETERNITY!
DURING THAT TIME, EVERYTHING I'VE EVER CARED FOR OR ACCOMPLISHED HAS FALLEN INTO RUIN! EVERYONE I'VE EVER LOVED NOW LIES DEAD.
MY LIFE HAS BEEN A FAILURE.
I WELCOME ITS END!
MAR-VELL, WHAT TRANSPIRES HERE?
I'M NOT SURE I COULD EXPLAIN...

...SO I'LL NOT TRY. WHAT OF THE OTHER AVENGERS?
STILL BACK AT THE OTHER SHIP, FIGHTING.

BY THE STARS, I YET LIVE!
BUT WHERE AM I?

AYE, EVEN THOUGH WE HAVE SHATTERED THE VILLAIN'S MASTER PLAN, HIS HORDES STILL STAND A THREAT TO EARTH'S SAFETY.
THEN WE'D BEST RETURN IMMEDIATELY TO AID THEM.
WHAT SHALL WE DO ABOUT WARLOCK?

IN A PLACE YOU HAVE LONG SOUGHT, A LAND OF PEACE.
GAMORA! PIP! THEN I TRULY AM IN...

NOTHING! THERE IS NOTHING WE CAN DO FOR ONE WHO HAS MADE THE ULTIMATE SACRIFICE FOR A WORLD HE ONCE CALLED HOME.
YET, SHED NO TEARS OF SORROW FOR HIM, AVENGERS.

...THE SOUL GEM!
HERE, WE ARE AS ONE. CAN YOU NOT FEEL THE COLLECTIVE MEMORY AND HEART WE ALL SHARE?

MINUTES AGO I SAW, HEARD, AND FELT A MOMENT I MAY NEVER TRULY UNDERSTAND, YET THIS MUCH WAS CLEAR TO ME:
FOR THE FIRST TIME IN HIS LONG AND TORTURED LIFE...

ADAM, CAN YOU NOT FEEL THE ABSENCE OF THE SHADOWS... FEEL THE LIGHT WHICH BURNS WITHIN US ALL...?
WHAT SHE'S TRYING TO SAY IS THAT THINGS ARE ALL RIGHT HERE.
THEY DON'T EVEN MIND MY PRESENCE.

...ADAM WARLOCK IS AT PEACE.

YES... IT'S TRUE! I CAN AT LAST FEEL THEM.
THERE'S AUTOLYCUS... KRA-TOR... THE BLACK KNIGHTS... WHISP'R... EVEN PART OF THE STAR THIEF... AND MANY OTHERS FROM BEFORE MY TIME.
THEY'RE... WE'RE ALL HERE TOGETHER... TRULY TOGETHER, FOR OUR HEARTS ARE OPEN BOOKS, AND THIS ATMOSPHERE BREEDS UNDERSTANDING AND MUTES THE EGO.
HERE WE ARE ALL ONE AND IN THIS ONENESS THERE CAN ONLY BE...
...LOVE.
WHILE, BACK IN THE REAL WORLD OF HARSH SHADOWS AND SHARP ANGLES, CAPTAIN MARVEL AND THE AVENGERS STILL FACE THE PERIL OF THANOS, A SITUATION TO BE RESOLVED WITH THE AID OF...
SPIDER-MAN and the THING... IN THE PAGES OF THE LATEST MARVEL TWO-IN-ONE ANNUAL...NOW ON SALE!

TWO-IN-ONE ANNUAL
2
1977
02348
60¢
CC
MARVEL COMICS GROUP TM
KING-SIZE ANNUAL!
ALL NEW!
MARVEL TWO-IN-ONE TM
PRESENTS
THE THING
AND
SPIDER-MAN ®
APPROVED BY THE COMICS CODE AUTHORITY
TO DUEL A MAD GOD!
TM
FEATURING:
THE AVENGERS
CAPTAIN MARVEL
& THE EPIC VILLAINY OF THANOS!

Stan Lee PRESENTS: The THING™ and SPIDER-MAN® ▫▫TOGETHER
JIM STARLIN STORY & ART / JOE RUBINSTEIN FINISHED ART / ANNETTE K., LETTERER PETRA G., COLORIST / ARCHIE GOODWIN EDITOR
DEATH WATCH!
WAIT!! DON'T READ THIS STORY UNTIL AFTER YOU CHECK OUT AVENGERS ANNUAL #7, NOW ON SALE.
IT'S 3 AM, YOU ARE ASLEEP AND YOUR NAME IS PETER PARKER.
USUALLY YOUR SLEEP IS THE TOTAL SURRENDER OF THE BONE WEARY.
BUT ALAS, TONIGHT'S REST IS NOT TO BE SO.
THIS EVENING YOUR SLUMBER IS TO BE INVADED BY A GIGANTIC SPACE ARK FLANKED BY SMALLER SHIPS.
YOU ARE DISTURBED AS THIS VISION CONTINUES, FOR YOU SUDDENLY REALIZE THAT LESS THAN AN HOUR AGO WITHIN THIS VESSEL...

...THE **AVENGERS** BATTLED SIDE-BY-SIDE WITH **CAPTAIN MARVEL** AND A BEING CALLED **WARLOCK,** WHOM YOU'VE MET ONCE BEFORE.

YOU WATCH HOW THEY FOUGHT FOR THEIR WORLD AGAINST A BIZARRE COLLECTION OF **ALIEN CRIMINALS** FROM THROUGHOUT THE GALAXY...

...AND YOU SENSE THE **HOPELESSNESS** OF THEIR POSITION, OUTNUMBERED **TWENTY** TO **ONE.**

ONCE INSIDE THE ARK, MAR-VEL MANAGED TO DESTROY A DEVICE WHICH WOULD HAVE SET OUR SUN NOVA, BUT THEN COLLAPSED FROM THE EFFORT IT REQUIRED.
THIS LEFT THE MAN CALLED ADAM WARLOCK ALONE TO FACE THE AWESOME MIGHT OF THANOS, WORSHIP-PER OF DEATH.

YOUR HEART BREAKS AS YOU WATCH HOW THE VALIANT GOLDEN WARRIOR WAS BRUTAL-LY CUT DOWN...

...THEN BLAZES IN NEW HOPE AS YOU SEE HOW THOR ENGAGED THE MASSIVE TITAN, WHILE...

...IRON MAN BLASTED THE SYNTHETIC POWER GEM WHICH POWERED THE VILLAIN'S STAR-BURSTING WEAPONRY.
THIS JEWEL, YOU REALIZE, WAS THE END PRODUCT OF COMBINING THE MIGHT OF THE FIVE GEMS OF POWER WHOSE SOLE SURVIVING MATE IS WARLOCK'S SOUL GEM.

THANOS REALIZED HIS MAIN SCHEME HAD FAILED AND PROMPTLY TELEPORTED OUT OF THE REACH OF THE WRATHFUL AVENGERS TO INITIATE HIS SECONDARY PLAN OF ATTACK.*
*ALL THIS TRANSPIRED IN AVENGERS ANNUAL #7--ARCHIE.

SUDDENLY YOU REALIZE YOUR REST IS NOT BEING DISTURBED BY NIGHTMARES OF YOUR OWN CREATION, BUT THAT ALL YOU HAVE EXPERIENCED IS PART OF A MENTAL CALL FOR AID BY THE AVENGER, MOON-DRAGON.

A CALL YOU KNOW YOU MUST ANSWER, BUT ONLY AFTER YOU HAVE THE COMPLETE STORY.

YOUR MIND RETURNS TO THE ORIGINAL SPACE ARK.

YOU SEE HOW THANOS' STRATEGIC RETREAT HAD RETURNED HIM TO THIS INITIAL BATTLEGROUND AND YOU SHUDDER AT THE SMILE HE WORE.

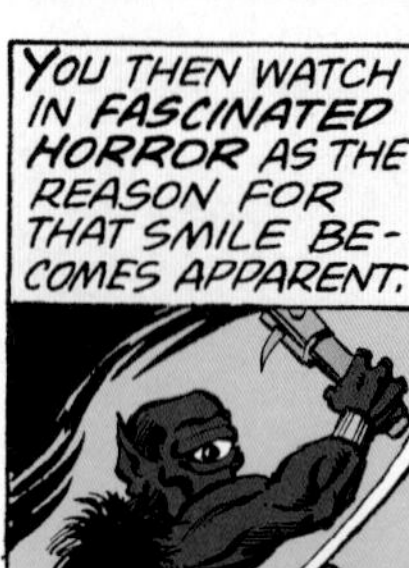
YOU THEN WATCH IN FASCINATED HORROR AS THE REASON FOR THAT SMILE BE-COMES APPARENT.

UNDER HIS AID AND DIRECTION HIS ARMY OF AL-IEN THRALLS, WHO UP UNTIL THAT POINT HAD BEEN A DISORGANIZED, INEFFECTUAL MOB--

--WAS SUDDENLY TRANSFORMED INTO A WELL-OILED FIGHTING MACH-INE. AVENGERS DROPPED LIKE FLIES UNDER THE ASSAULT.

THEN SUDDENLY, BEFORE YOU HAVE TRULY GRASPED THE REALITIES OF THE STRUGGLE YOU WITNESS...

...IT COMES TO AN END.

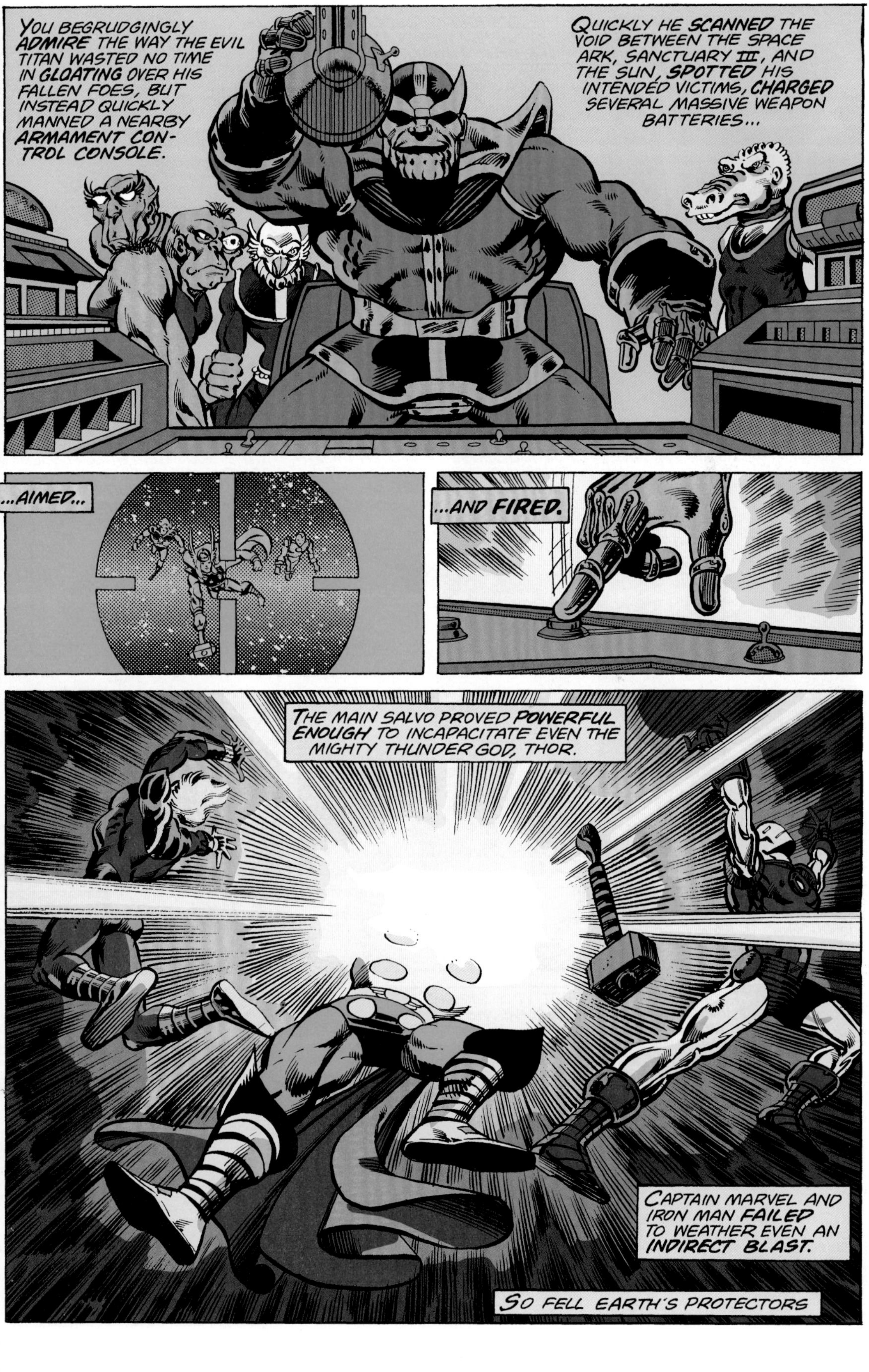

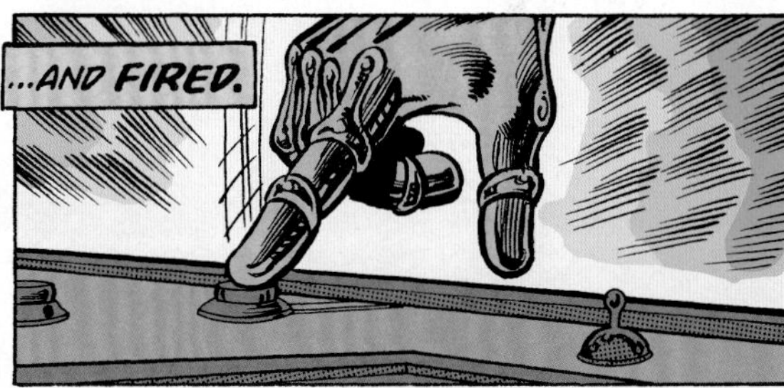

THE MAIN SALVO PROVED POWERFUL ENOUGH TO INCAPACITATE EVEN THE MIGHTY THUNDER GOD, THOR.

CAPTAIN MARVEL AND IRON MAN FAILED TO WEATHER EVEN AN INDIRECT BLAST.

SO FELL EARTH'S PROTECTORS

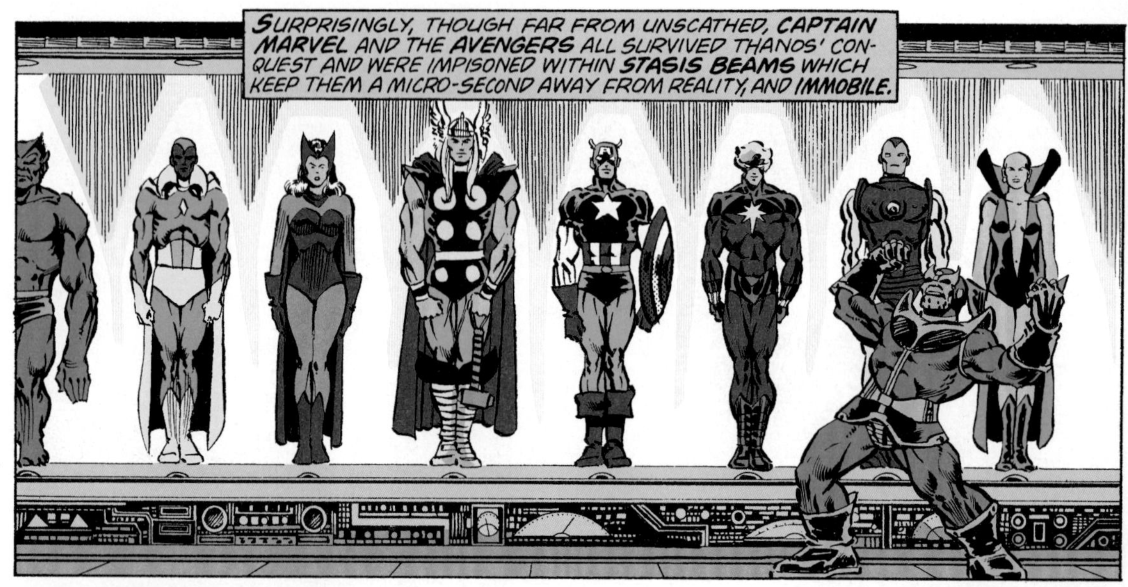
SURPRISINGLY, THOUGH FAR FROM UNSCATHED, CAPTAIN MARVEL AND THE AVENGERS ALL SURVIVED THANOS' CONQUEST AND WERE IMPISONED WITHIN STASIS BEAMS WHICH KEEP THEM A MICRO-SECOND AWAY FROM REALITY, AND IMMOBILE.

THE ONLY FATALITY WAS ADAM WARLOCK.
HIS BODY WAS BROUGHT BEFORE THANOS, WHO WRENCHED THE SOUL GEM FROM THE FALLEN HERO'S BROW. AT THIS YOU SHUDDER.

FOR YOU SENSE THAT EVEN THOUGH IT HAS NOT THE POWER TO EXTINGUISH ALL THE STARS OF THE NIGHT AS THANOS ORIGINALLY HOPED TO DO...

...THE SOUL GEM STILL POSSESSES THE MIGHT TO BLOW OUT THE STAR SOL, OUR OWN SUN.

PERHAPS THAT WILL BE ENOUGH...
...TO APPEASE DEATH.

OH MY GOD!
IT'S ALL TRUE. I KNOW IT IS.
SOMEHOW, WHILE IMPRISONED, MOONDRAGON BEAMED A TELEPATHIC SOS MY SPIDER SENSE PICKED UP IN MY SLEEP.

BUT WHY DID SHE CHOOSE ME?
I'M NOT EQUIPPED FOR THIS SORT OF THING.
I'M NO POWERHOUSE LIKE THOR OR STAR JUMPER LIKE CAPTAIN MARVEL.

I'M ONLY YOUR TYPICAL NEIGHBORHOOD SPIDER-MAN.

MEANWHILE, COUNTLESS LIGHT YEARS AWAY ON THE EDGE OF INFIN-ITY...

...A VOICE IS HEARD
IT GOES BADLY.

DEATH'S GAME PIECE AT THIS POINT HAS THE SUPERIOR POSITION, LORD CHAOS.
WE ARE AL-READY FORCED TO PLACE OUR RESERVES INTO PLAY.

YET WILL EVEN THEY BE ENOUGH TO WIN THE DAY FOR US, MAS-TER ORDER?
THE STILL ONE HAS NEVER HAD SUCH A STRONG HAND BEFORE.

BUT SO HAVE WE IN THE FORM OF SPIDER-MAN AND THE MAN HE IS DES-TINED TO ALLY HIMSELF WITH, BENJAMIN GRIMM.
LET US HOPE THEY ARE ENOUGH.

OKAY, PARKER, HERE YOU ARE ALL SUITED UP AND READY FOR ACTION.
THE ONLY TROUBLE IS...
...YOUR WEBS AREN'T LONG ENOUGH TO SWING YOU WHERE YOU HAVE TO GO.

FACE IT, PAL, THIS IS ONE TIME YOU CAN'T PLAY THE LONE WOLF.
YOU NEED HELP.
YOU NEED SOMEONE WHO HAS ACCESS TO A SPACE-CRAFT.

SO, WHO SHOULD YOU TURN TO AT A TIME LIKE THIS?
WELL, WHO ELSE OTHER THAN THOSE FRIENDLY FOLKS OVER AT...

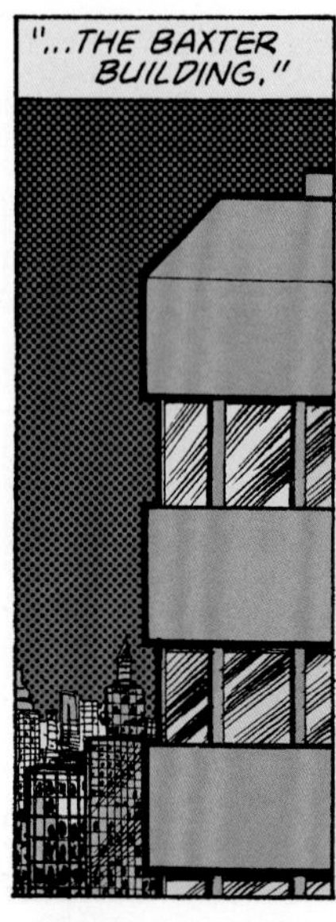
"...THE BAXTER BUILDING."

BLAST IT, THAT STINKING VAMPIRE GOT THE PRIEST.

WHAT ARE THEY GOING TO DO NOW?
SALEM LOT

AAAAAAAAAHH!

PITTUI!

WHO?!
SPIDER-MAN! I SHOULD HAVE KNOWN.
HIYA, BENJY!

DON'T 'BENJY' ME, YOU NO-GOOD INSECT!
BUT...
DO YA GOT ANY IDEA HOW MUCH THAT CIGAR YOU JUST MADE ME SWALLOW COST?

OR HOW BAD IT TASTED?
BESIDES, REED SPENT A WAD OF DOUGH ON SECURITY DEVICES TO KEEP RIFF-RAFF LIKE YOU OUT.
BEN...

AIN'T YOU GOT NO RESPECT FOR MACHINERY? CAN'T YOU TAKE A HINT?
WE DON'T LIKE YOU JUST POPPING OUT OF NOWHERE AND SCARING THE DAYLIGHTS OUT OF US.
BUT...

IT'S EMBARASSING, AND THINK WHAT IT DOES TO OUR IMAGES.
WE'VE GOT FANS OUT THERE YOU KNOW.

WHAT WOULD THEY THINK IF...
SHUT UP!

...PLEASE.
WHAT'S WRONG, WEB-HEAD? GOT TROUBLES?
YEAH.
WELL, YOU'VE COME TO THE RIGHT PLACE THEN.
WE'RE ALL EARS AND HELPING HANDS HERE AT THE FANTASTIC FOUR.

BOY, AM I GLAD OF THAT.
HOW ABOUT USING ONE OF THOSE HELPING HANDS TO POUR US SOME JAVA.
I'VE GOT ONE DOOZEY OF A STORY TO LAY ON YOU, AND COFFEE WILL HELP.

TWO CUPS OF CAFFEINE AND A 'DOOZEY OF A STORY' LATER...
SPIDEY...
...THAT'S THE CRAZIEST STORY I EVER HEARD.

WHAT HAVE YOU BEEN SMOKING, KID?
OLD TENNIS SHOES?

HONESTLY, BEN, I'M NOT SNOWING YOU. I'M IN A FIX AND...
...YOU'RE THE ONLY PERSON I KNOW THAT I CAN TURN TO.

ALL RIGHT. YOU'VE ALWAYS BEEN PRETTY STRAIGHT WITH ME IN THE PAST, SO I GUESS I BETTER CHECK IT OUT.

C'MON, REED'S GOT THIS SPACE SHUTTLE CRAFT HE WANTS ME TO TEST-PILOT WHEN I GET A CHANCE.
NOW'S AS GOOD A TIME AS ANY.

WHERE EXACTLY IS THE GIANT SPACE ARK?
JUST RIGHT OF THE EARTH, FACING THE SUN.
OH, GREAT--AIN'T YOU THE REGULAR NAVIGATIONAL TECHNICIAN.

SORRY...
OKAY, OKAY. IF IT'S UP THERE, THIS CRATE'S GOT TRACKING SYSTEMS THAT WILL PIN IT DOWN.

IF? STILL HAVE YOUR DOUBTS, THEN?
ABOUT YOUR STORY? PERISH FORBID SUCH A THOUGHT.

HOW COULD ANYONE DOUBT THE WORD OF A MAN IN BLUE AND RED LEOTARDS WHO CRAWLS ON WALLS?

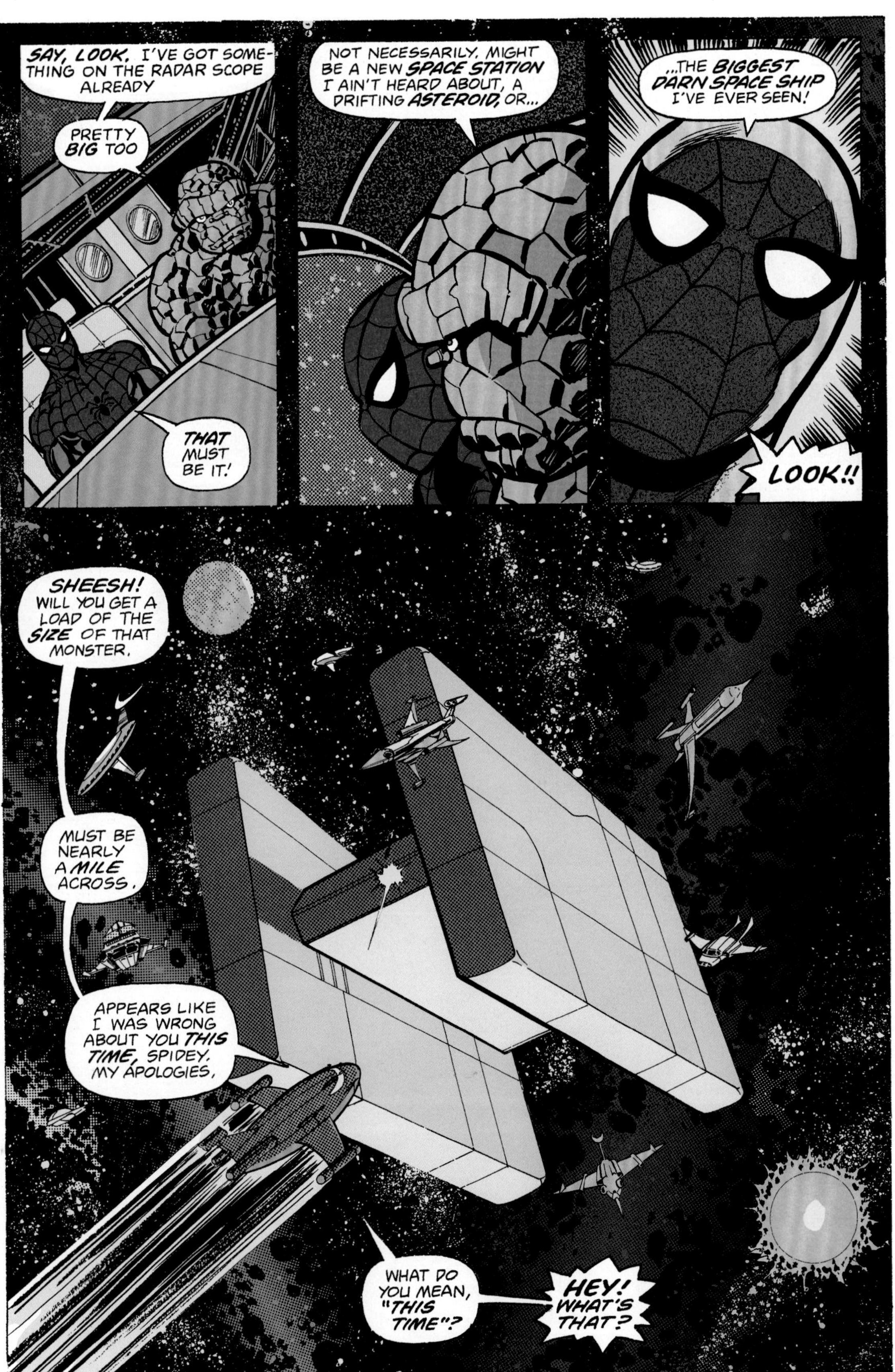
SAY, LOOK. I'VE GOT SOMETHING ON THE RADAR SCOPE ALREADY
PRETTY BIG TOO
THAT MUST BE IT!
NOT NECESSARILY. MIGHT BE A NEW SPACE STATION I AIN'T HEARD ABOUT, A DRIFTING ASTEROID, OR...
...THE BIGGEST DARN SPACE SHIP I'VE EVER SEEN!
LOOK!!
SHEESH! WILL YOU GET A LOAD OF THE SIZE OF THAT MONSTER.
MUST BE NEARLY A MILE ACROSS.
APPEARS LIKE I WAS WRONG ABOUT YOU THIS TIME, SPIDEY. MY APOLOGIES.
WHAT DO YOU MEAN, "THIS TIME"?
HEY! WHAT'S THAT?

TRACTOR BEAM! WE'VE BEEN SNAGGED-- GETTING PULLED INTO THE MAIN SHIP.

WELL, I'VE BEEN THROUGH THIS SORT OF THING BEFORE. ONCE THIS AIRLOCK WE'RE BEING DRAGGED INTO IS SEALED OFF, WE CAN EXPECT TO BE ATTACKED BY A PACK OF GOONS.

THESE TYPES OF GUYS PLAY ROUGH, SO YOU JUST SIT BACK AND LET ME HANDLE THINGS.

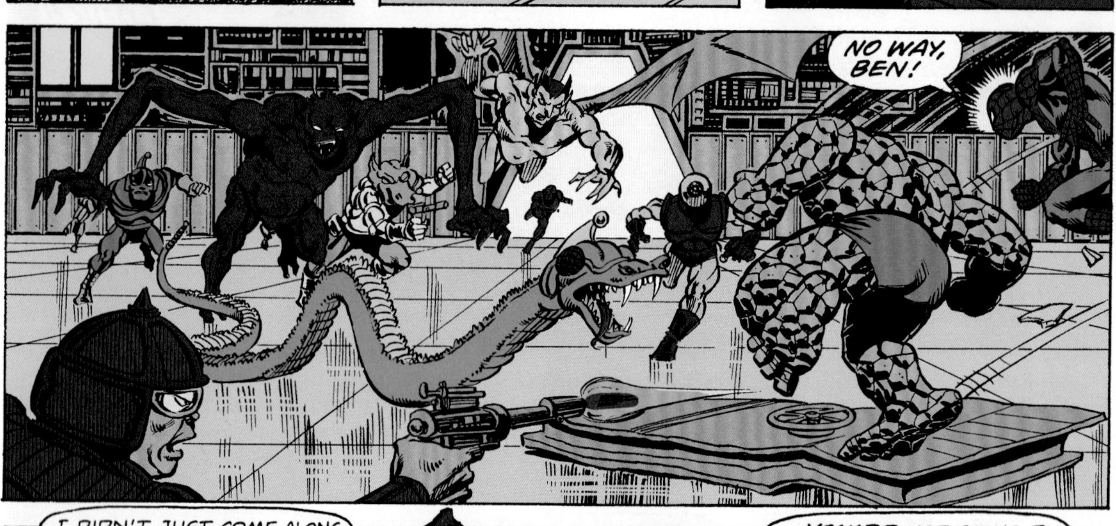
NO WAY, BEN!

I DIDN'T JUST COME ALONG FOR THE RIDE, AND...
...YOU'RE NOT GOING TO HOG ALL THE FUN!
SAY, AIN'T MONSTER BASHING A BIT OUT OF YOUR LINE?

MOST DEFINITELY.
BUT THERE'S PLENTY OF SMALL FRIES FOR ME TO HANDLE.

THEY'RE NOT MUCH WORSE THAN EARTH THUGS WITH JAZZY HARDWARE,

SO I'LL KEEP THEM OFF YOUR BACK WHILE YOU TAKE CARE OF LARGER MATTERS.
SEE?

YEAH, THANKS!
GOT TO ADMIT THESE "LARGER MATTERS" ARE KEEPING ME KIND'A BUSY...

...BUT IT'S ONLY A TEMPORARY CONDITION.

SEE?

BEN! SOMEONE CUT OFF THE GRAVITY IN THIS CHAMBER!

THAT WAS THANOS!

I'D RECOGNIZE THAT VOICE ANYWHERE THIS SIDE OF THE GRAVE.

SPIDEY, I THINK WE'RE REALLY IN FOR IT NOW.

WE SURE ARE! NEITHER WEB-HEAD OR MYSELF ARE AT OUR BEST IN ZERO GRAVITY.
BLAST IT! THEY'VE ALREADY TAKEN OUT SPIDEY, WHICH MEANS IT'S ONLY A MATTER OF TIME BEFORE I'M...

...HEAAXXTS!

YET STILL ANOTHER ROUND GOES TO DEATH!

THE THING AND SPIDER-MAN HAVE BEEN AT LEAST TEMPORARILY TAKEN OUT OF PLAY.

OF COURSE, WE BOTH EXPECTED THIS TO HAPPEN

NEITHER WERE EVER MEANT TO CARRY THE DAY FOR US
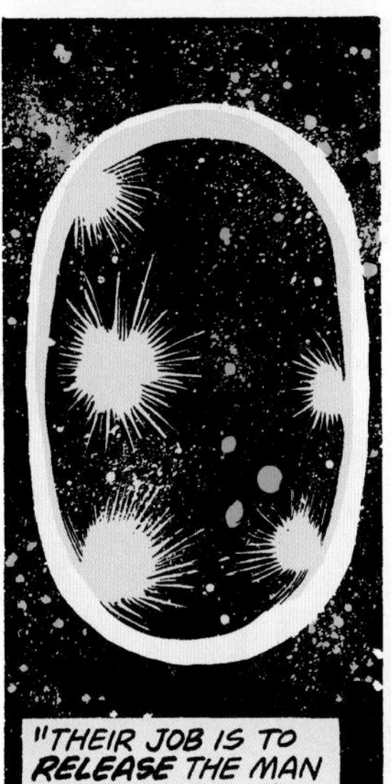
"THEIR JOB IS TO RELEASE THE MAN WHO WILL."

"HE MUST BE CALLED FORTH FROM A WORLD WITHIN A GEM."

"A WORLD OF GREEN HILLS AND EMERALD SKIES."

"OUR CHAMPION IS, OF COURSE, ADAM WARLOCK."

I JUST CAN'T BELIEVE IT!
LESS THAN AN HOUR AGO I WAS DYING FROM WOUNDS SUFFERED AT THANOS' HANDS.

NOW I FIND MYSELF ON THIS PARADISE-LIKE WORLD WITHIN MY SOUL GEM, WITHOUT A CARE OR WORRY TO PLAGUE ME.

BETTER STILL, I FIND MYSELF WITH FRIENDS I THOUGHT FOREVER LOST TO THE SPIRIT-DEVOURING POWER OF MY SOUL GEM.
GAMORA, IT'S SO GRAND TO BE WITH YOU AND PIP AGAIN.

IT'S EVEN GOOD SEEING MY OLD FOES WHO ALSO FELL VICTIM TO THE GEM'S HUNGER, FOR THEY ARE NO LONGER ENEMIES.

FOR HERE WE ALL SHARE THE SAME FEELINGS, THE SAME MEMORIES, THE SAME SOUL.
WITHIN THE GEM THERE IS NO ONE VICTIMIZING ANYONE, FOR SUCH MADNESS WOULD BE LIKE HARMING ONE'S SELF.
I NEVER DREAMT SUCH PEACE AND HAPPINESS COULD BE

I PRAY IT MAY LAST.

DARKNESS.

LIGHT.

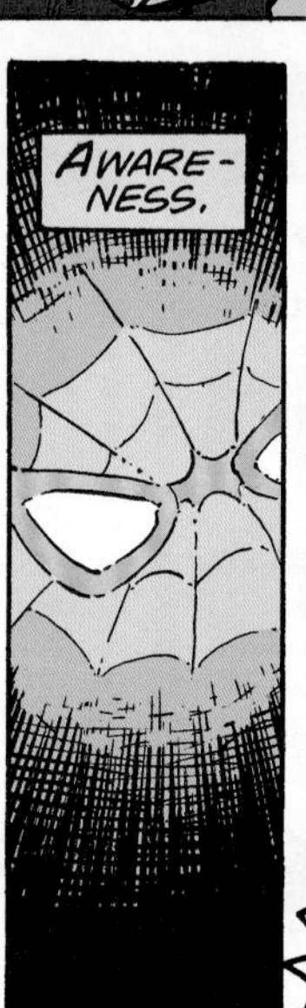
AWARENESS.

REALITY!
HOLY COW!

APTLY PUT, MY ARACHNID ADVERSARY.
THE POWER OF THANOS, DEVOTEE OF DEATH, IS INDEED AWE-INSPIRING, IS IT NOT?
BEFORE YOU STANDS MUTE TESTIMONY OF MY MIGHT. BEHOLD MY HELPLESS CAPTIVES, THE ONCE INVINCIBLE AVENGERS.
MY THRALLS ARE BUSY PREPARING SIMILAR ACCOMMODATIONS FOR YOU, BUT UNTIL THEN...
...I THOUGHT YOU MIGHT ENJOY BEING SHOWN THE FATE YOU ARE ESCAPING BY BECOMING PART OF MY, SHALL WE SAY, TROPHY COLLECTION.

WHAT I'D REALLY ENJOY IS PUTTING MY FIST IN YOUR FACE, CREEP!
BEN, LET'S HEAR HIM OUT.

HA! I LIKE YOUR FRIEND, BEN GRIMM. HE'S A SCHEMER.
HE HOPES THAT ENCOURAGING MY NATURAL LONG-WINDEDNESS WILL GIVE HIM TIME TO PLAN...

...PERHAPS EVEN GIVE HIM SOME IDEA ON HOW TO CIRCUMVENT MY GRAND PLANS.
ALAS, POOR SPIDER-MAN, IT IS MY SAD DUTY TO INFORM YOU THAT SUCH DREAMS ARE FUTILE.

FOR THANOS NOW HOLDS THE SOUL GEM AND STANDS INVINCIBLE.

EVEN AS WE STAND HERE, MY ARMY IS READYING ANOTHER STELLAR PROJECTOR WHICH WILL BEND THIS GEM'S POWER TO MY WILL.
THAT POWER WILL THEN BE FOCUSED ON YOUR SUN CAUSING IT TO GO...

...NOVA--AND DESTROY ALL LIFE IN YOUR SOLAR SYSTEM.

GOOD HEAVEN, MAN, WHY?

WHY, FOR DEATH...OF COURSE.

YEARS AGO, AFTER MY EXILE FROM TITAN, I MET AND FELL IN LOVE WITH THE PERSONIFICATION OF DEATH!
FOR A TIMELESS TIME I SERVED HER AND SHE AIDED ME IN MY SCHEMES.

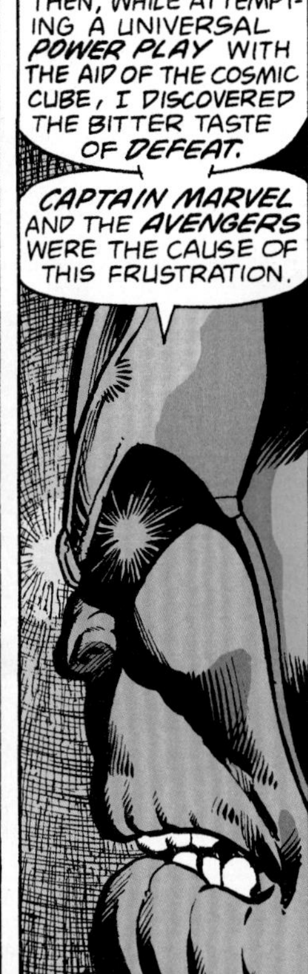
THEN, WHILE ATTEMPTING A UNIVERSAL POWER PLAY WITH THE AID OF THE COSMIC CUBE, I DISCOVERED THE BITTER TASTE OF DEFEAT.
CAPTAIN MARVEL AND THE AVENGERS WERE THE CAUSE OF THIS FRUSTRATION.
BECAUSE OF THEIR INTERFERENCE, DEATH BEGAN TO DOUBT MY WORTH AS A LOVER, AND EVENTUALLY ABANDONED ME.

BUT I SWORE TO REGAIN HER FAVOR WITH A STELLAR TOKEN OF MY LOVE, THE LIKES OF WHICH HAS NEVER BEFORE BEEN WITNESSED BY THE COSMOS!
MY OFFERING WOULD SHOW HER THAT I--ABOVE ALL OTHER BEINGS--DESERVED TO BE HER CHAMPION AND LOVER!

THAT IS WHY YOUR SOLAR SYSTEM MUST DIE!

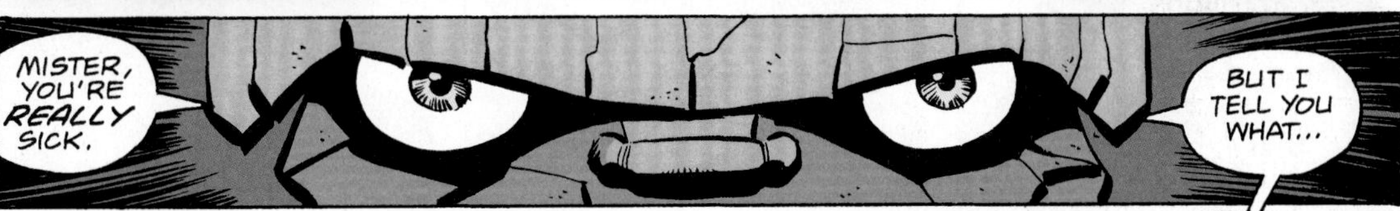
MISTER, YOU'RE REALLY SICK.
BUT I TELL YOU WHAT...

...DR. GRIMM HERE HAS GOT THE CURE FOR WHAT AILS YOU.
HIS WORLD-FAMOUS KNUCKLE KNOCK-OUT FORMULA!

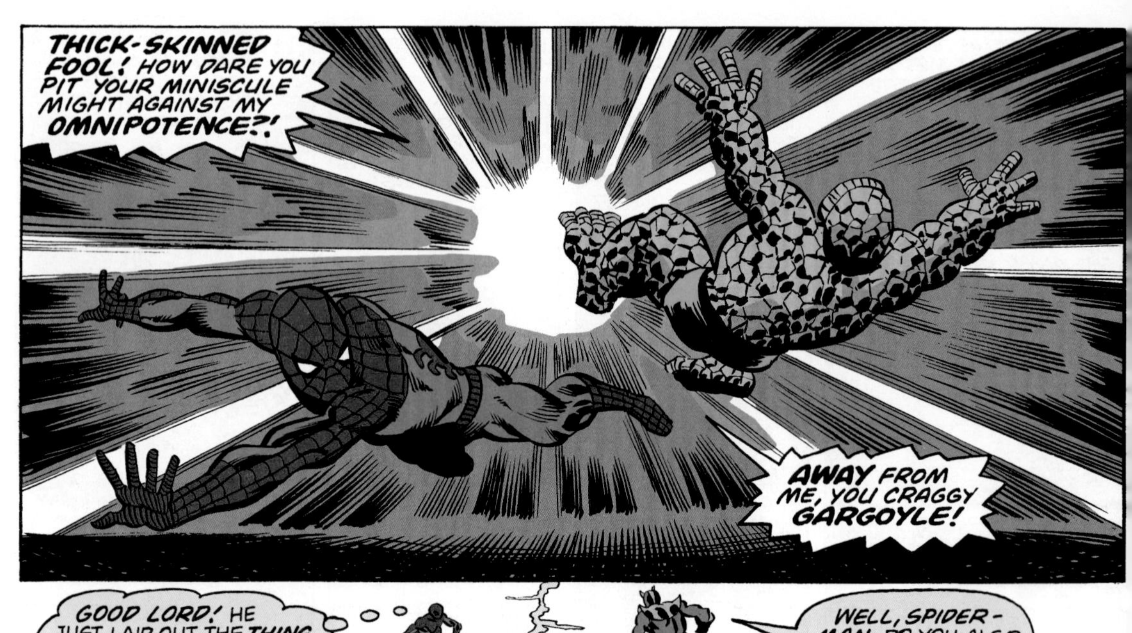
THICK-SKINNED FOOL! HOW DARE YOU PIT YOUR MINISCULE MIGHT AGAINST MY OMNIPOTENCE?!
AWAY FROM ME, YOU CRAGGY GARGOYLE!

GOOD LORD! HE JUST LAID OUT THE THING FOR THE TEN COUNT WITH-OUT EVEN WORKING UP A SWEAT!
WELL, SPIDER-MAN, DO YOU ALSO CRAVE A TASTE OF MY MIGHT?

PETER, OLD BOY, YOU'VE REALLY STEPPED INTO IT UP TO YOUR NECK THIS TIME!
HERE YOU ARE FACING A MONSTER WHO JUST CREAMED THE AVENGERS, BEN GRIMM, AND CAPTAIN MARVEL --AND NOW PLANS TO BLOW OUT THE SUN!

FACE IT, PARKER--THIS IS WAY OUT OF YOUR LEAGUE!
YOU WERE PUT TOGETHER TO FIGHT CHEAP HOODS AND COSTUMED CRAZIES!

THERE'S NOTHING IN THE SPIDER-MAN MANUAL ABOUT FIGHTING STAR BURSTING DEMI-GODS!
I DON'T BELONG HERE...

...AND I'M NOT GOING TO STAY!
WHAT?! WHAT ARE YOU DOING?
LEAVING!
THIS IS THE AVENGERS' HASSLE.

THEY KNOW HOW TO GET OUT OF THESE SITUATIONS.
DON'T THEY?
THEY'LL SAVE THE DAY YET
WON'T THEY?

GUARDS! AFTER THAT CRAVEN, COSTUMED CLOWN!
BRING ME BACK HIS HEAD!

NOW WHERE DO I GO? WHAT DO I DO?
EVEN IF I MAKE IT BACK TO THE THING'S SHIP I'D NEVER BE ABLE TO FIGURE OUT HOW TO FLY IT!

BUT I CAN'T STAY HERE! ALL I'LL ACCOMPLISH IS GETTING KILLED BY STICKING AROUND!

BUT IF THANOS SUCCEEDS IN HIS PLANS, WHAT GOOD WILL RUNNING BACK TO EARTH DO?
NONE!

REMAIN OR RUN, IT LOOKS LIKE DEAD SPIDER FOR DINNER.
OKAY! SO I STAY...AND DO WHAT?

THANOS WOULD MAKE MINCE-MEAT OUT OF ME IN ANY KIND OF DIRECT CONFRONTATION.
IN FACT, HE'D PROBABLY SWEEP THE FLOOR WITH ANYONE ABOARD...

...EXCEPT MAYBE THOR.
LOOKS LIKE THAT'S GOT TO BE MY PLAN. I'LL HAVE TO TURN AROUND AND FREE THE MAN WITH THE HAMMER...

...AND TRY TO AVOID GETTING TOO DEAD DOING SO.
WHEW!
THAT WAS SOME BLIND PANIC NUMBER I JUST RAN MYSELF THROUGH. SURE GLAD IT PASSED.
MAYBE I'M GETTING TOO OLD FOR THIS KIND OF GIG?
I'LL HAVE TO DO SOME HEAVY THINKING ALONG THOSE LINES LATER.

THAT IS, IF THERE IS A LATER FOR ME.

FOR A MOMENT THERE, MASTER ORDER, I FEARED THE YOUTH'S SPIRIT WAS GOING TO FAIL US.

HIS INSTINCT FOR SELF-PRESERVATION NEARLY KEPT HIM FROM HIS CHOSEN FATE.
I HAD FORESEEN THIS POSSIBILITY, LORD CHAOS --BUT HAD FAITH IN THIS NOBLE EARTHMAN'S STRONG HEART WINNING OUT IN THE END.

FOR WAS IT NOT US WHO CHOSE TO ENDOW HIM WITH THE DESTINY OF BEING...

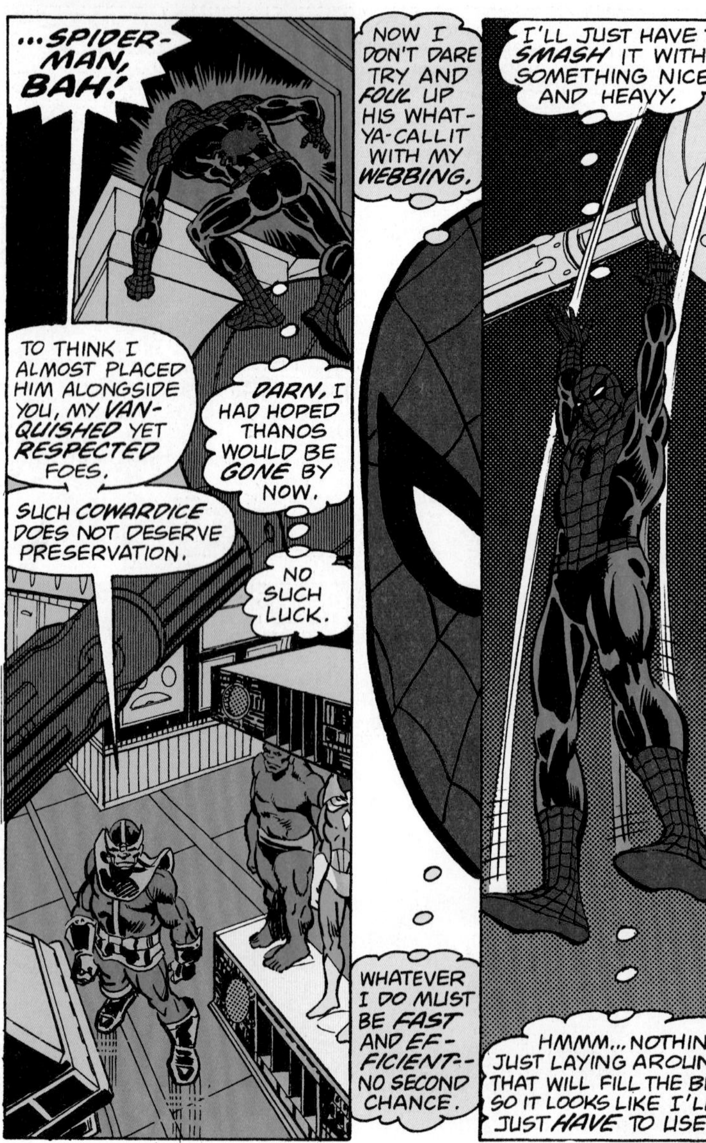
...SPIDER-MAN, BAH!
TO THINK I ALMOST PLACED HIM ALONGSIDE YOU, MY VAN-QUISHED YET RESPECTED FOES.
SUCH COWARDICE DOES NOT DESERVE PRESERVATION.
DARN, I HAD HOPED THANOS WOULD BE GONE BY NOW.
NO SUCH LUCK.
NOW I DON'T DARE TRY AND FOUL UP HIS WHAT-YA-CALLIT WITH MY WEBBING.
WHATEVER I DO MUST BE FAST AND EF-FICIENT-- NO SECOND CHANCE.
I'LL JUST HAVE TO SMASH IT WITH SOMETHING NICE AND HEAVY.
HMMM... NOTHING JUST LAYING AROUND THAT WILL FILL THE BILL, SO IT LOOKS LIKE I'LL JUST HAVE TO USE...

...MYSELF!

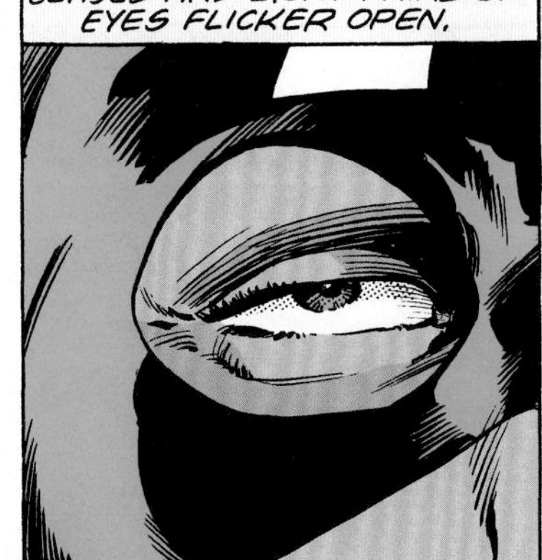

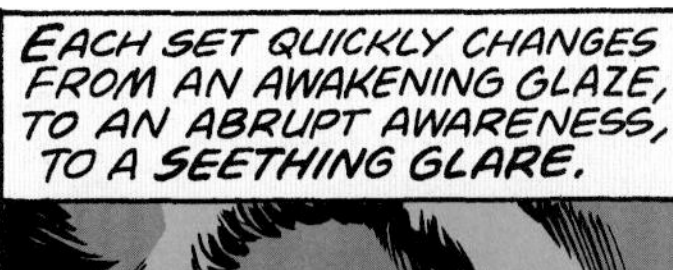

BUT IT IS!

THE AVENGERS ARE FREE!

TO ARMS, AVENGERS!

THE TIME HATH COME TO LIVE UP TO OUR PROUD NAME!

YEAH! THIS ONE'S FOR WARLOCK!

NO!

UNHAND ME, YOU PITIFUL LOUTS!
YOU MAY HAVE SUCCEEDED IN ESCAPING IMPRISONMENT--
--BUT I ASSURE YOU THAT DEFEATING THANOS, THE RIGHT HAND OF DEATH, IS ANOTHER MATTER ENTIRELY!

EVEN NOW, MY ARMY OF THRALLS IS RUSHING TO MY SIDE.
TOGETHER WE WILL DEAL WITH YOU AS I SHOULD HAVE DONE ORIGINALLY!

TAKE NO PRISONERS!
YOU HEARD THE MAN, AVENGERS!
IT'S DO OR DIE THIS TIME!
SO TEAR INTO THEM BUT GOOD!

HEY, PURPLE PUSS-- REMEMBER ME?
IT'S THE BASHFUL, BLUE-EYED THING COME FOR A PIECE OF YOUR TAIL!
AS HAS THOR, THE GOD OF THUNDER!

THE CHAMBER ROCKS WITH THE SOUND OF BATTLE AS MACHINERY, BONES, AND CONSCIOUSNESS FALL VICTIM TO THE WILD MELEE WHICH SPRINGS TO A LIFE OF ITS OWN.
IN THE VERY EYE OF THIS STORM OF BODIES, THE ASGARDIAN DEITY AND THE FANTASTIC FOUR'S STRONGEST MEMBER STRUGGLE TO KEEP THE VILLAINOUS DESCENDANT OF OLYMPUS FROM TURNING THE SURROUNDING CHAOS INTO AN ORGANIZED AND EFFECTIVE KILLING FORCE DIRECTED AT EARTH'S DEFENDERS.

STAY ON THE OFFENSIVE, AVENGERS! KEEP THEM SCATTERED ABOUT!
IF THEY GET THEIR ACT TOGETHER, WE'RE FINISHED!
SO LESS TALK, GOOD CAPTAIN, AND MORE OLD FASHIONED JAW BUSTING!
SAY, AERIAL RECONNAISSANCE, ANYTHING TO REPORT?
ENEMY BUILD-UP AT THREE O'CLOCK!
SOMEONE BREAK IT UP!
FEAR NOT, MAR-VELL, I SENSE THE VISION HAS ALL UNDER CONTROL...
...WITH THE AID OF HIS SOLAR-POWERED EYE BLASTS!

THEN WE NEED ONLY WORRY ABOUT THE DANGER'S HEAD--FOR ITS LIMBS HAVE BEEN RENDERED HARMLESS!
SURRENDER, VILLAIN! THY CAUSE IS LOST!
THOOOM!
NEVER! AS LONG AS LIFE REMAINS WITHIN ME, HOPE STILL REMAINS FOR THE CAUSE OF DEATH!
KA-TAM!
I'D NOT WAGER HEAVILY ON A FAVORABLE OUTCOME TO THIS BATTLE, TITAN...
...FOR YOU FACE THOR, MIGHTIEST OF FABLED ASGARD'S WARRIORS...
...AND THE THING, IDOL OF MILLIONS!
TOGETHER...
...WE SPELL TROUBLE!
KAROOOOOOOM!

FOOLS!!
YOUR COMBINED BLOWS MERELY SERVED TO GAIN ME THE DISTANCE NEEDED TO TURN MY DESTRUCTIVE EYE BEAMS UPON YOU!
DIE, LIFE-LOVING SIMPLETONS!

THE THING HAS FALLEN AND...
...A FEW MORE SUCH BLASTS WILL HAVE THOR JOINING HIM.

YOU ARE CORRECT IN THAT ASSUMPTION, MORTAL, BUT SOLE RESPONSIBILITY IS NOT YOUR BURDEN.
THERE IS ANOTHER...

"...MERE YARDS AND A WORLD AWAY."
ARGH! MY HEAD!
ADAM! WHAT'S WRONG?

BEING PULLED... FORCED... DRAWN FROM THE GEM!
BEING CALLED BACK TO REALITY FOR ONE LAST TASK!

ONE LAST MISSION OF VENGEANCE!

THE FINAL LAYER IS PRIMED. IT NOW ONLY REMAINS FOR THE INTER-MEDIARY, SPIDER-MAN, TO FACILITATE HIS RELEASE.

THE OLD SPIDER-SENSE IS GOING CRAZY. WHY?
I SAW THAT GOON ATTACKING WITHOUT ITS AID.

WAIT! IT FEELS DIFFERENT THIS TIME... LIKE IT'S TRYING TO LEAD ME TOWARD SOME-THING...

...AND THAT SOMETHING HAS GOT TO BE WARLOCK'S SOUL GEM, ENCASED IN THAT GLASS GLOBE!

HE HAS AT LAST REALIZED HIS GOAL, BUT...
...WILL HE REACH IT?
THAT, I'M AFRAID, LORD CHAOS--
--IS BEYOND EVEN OUR ABILITIES TO FORE-SEE.

WONDER WHEN THANOS HAD TIME TO POP THE GEM IN THAT GLOBE?
WELL, IT DOESN'T MATTER. I'M NOT SURE WHY, BUT THE ONLY THING THAT COUNTS NOW...

...IS GETTING THAT JEWEL OUT OF THAT FANCY FISH BOWL.
UGH!

CAN'T BE STOPPED NOW...
...TOO MUCH AT STAKE...
...BILLIONS OF LIVES RIDING ON ME...

...BUT I CAN'T SEE ANYTHING BUT STARS ENGULFING ME...STARS ABOUT TO DIE...
NO! GOT TO SWING MY ARMS ABOUT...KNOW GLOBE IS SOMEWHERE... IN FRONT OF ME...

I DID IT!
I DID IT!
I DID IT!

I,..HEY, WHAT THE DEVIL **DID** I DO?
YOU HAVE SUCCEEDED IN RELEASING ME-- THE **ULTIMATE AVENGER.**
WHO ARE YOU? WHAT DO YOU MEAN?
THANOS KNOWS ME AND MY **PURPOSE!** IS THAT NOT SO, EVIL ONE?
BY THE GREAT NEBULA! IT CAN-NOT BE **YOU!**
I SAW YOU **DIE!** I **KILLED YOU!**

THAT YOU DID, VILE SERPENT. YET **I** COULD NOT REST WHILE YOU REMAINED A THREAT TO **MY UNIVERSE!**

NO-- STAY BACK!

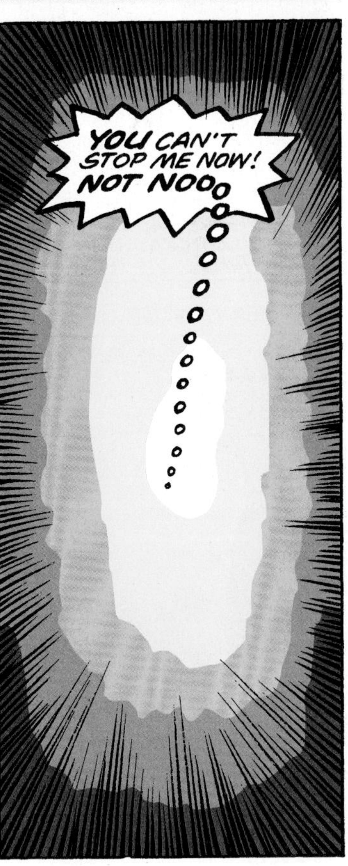
YOU CAN'T STOP ME NOW! **NOT NOOooooooooooooooo...**

THE EXPLOSIVE FLASH **BLINDS** EVERYONE MOMENTARILY. BUT EVEN WHEN THEIR VISION CLEARS, **NONE** ARE QUITE SURE THEY SHOULD **BELIEVE** WHAT THEIR EYES SEE.

BEFORE THEM HAD STOOD **THANOS**, PROUD, POWERFUL, RUTHLESS, AND MERE HEART-BEATS FROM **VICTORY**. NOW IN THAT EXACT SPOT, MOMENTS LATER, STANDS THE MASSIVE TITAN TRANSFORMED INTO SOLID **GRANITE**.

...HE WAS BORN ON EARTH. HIS CREATORS MEANT HIM TO BE THE PROTOTYPE OF THAT PLANET'S FUTURE HUMANITY.
YET, STRANGELY, HE ALWAYS FELT OUT OF PLACE AT HOME, AND PREFERRED WANDERING AMONG THE STARS.

THAT IS WHY WE BURIED HIM HERE, WITH THE WOMAN HE MIGHT HAVE LOVED AND HIS ONE FRIEND.

I PITY HIM HIS LOT IN LIFE. FOR EVEN HERE AMIDST THE HEAVENS, ADAM WARLOCK NEVER TRULY FOUND A PLACE FOR HIMSELF.

IN HIS YOUTH, WHEREVER HE WENT HE WAS FOUND GUILTY OF INNOCENCE AND EVENTU-ALLY EXECUTED FOR THAT CRIME.

HE WAS ***RESURRECTED*** FROM THE ASHES FREE OF HIS CHILD-ISH INCULPABILITY, BUT HAUNTED BY CYNICISM WHICH REMAINED.

FINALLY HE FOUND LIGHT, LIFE AND TRUTH TO BE HIS ONLY VALUES, AND SO BE-CAME MISUNDERSTOOD AND ALONE.
IN THE END, WHILE PROTECTING THAT WHICH HE CHERISHED, HE DIED AS WE ARE ALL DESTINED TO DO.

I ONLY PRAY THAT WHEN MY TIME IS AT HAND, I'LL BE ABLE TO PASS AS HONORABLY AS HE.

WE WILL MOURN YOU, ADAM WARLOCK.
WE CAN DO NO MORE

HERE LIES
ADAM WARLOCK
GOD SLAYER, SAVIOR OF TWO WORLDS, AND TORMENTED SOUL.
MAY HE NOW BE AT PEACE.
1967 1977

LATER, ABOARD SANCTUARY III...

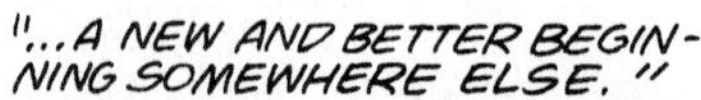

Warlock #9 cover
art by Jim Starlin & Alan Weiss

Warlock #9 cover production overlay used to facilitate the printed art's color-hold background

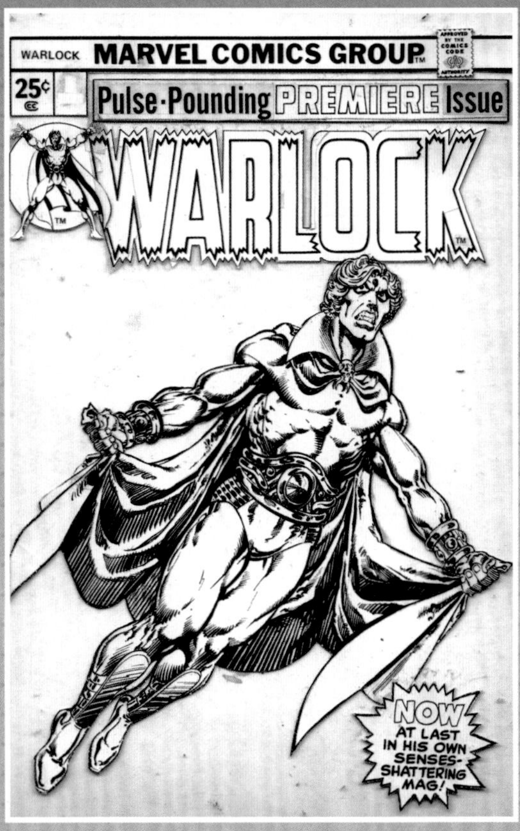

Strange Tales #181, page 13
art by Jim Starlin & Al Milgrom

Warlock #11, page 10
art by Jim Starlin & Steve Leialoha

Official Handbook of the Marvel Universe profile artwork by John Byrne, Josef Rubinstein & Andy Yanchus

Official Handbook of the Marvel Universe: Deluxe Edition profile artwork by Josef Rubinstein & Andy Yanchus

MARVEL COMICS GROUP
$2.00 CAN. $2.25
2 JAN
WARLOCK
SPECIAL EDITION

Warlock Special Edition #2 (1982) reprinted material from Strange Tales #180-181 and Warlock #9. Cover art by Jim Starlin.

Warlock #3 (1992) reprinted material from Warlock #10-12. Cover art by Jim Starlin.

Essential Marvel Two-In-One Vol. 2 TPB back-cover art by Jim Starlin & Tom Smith

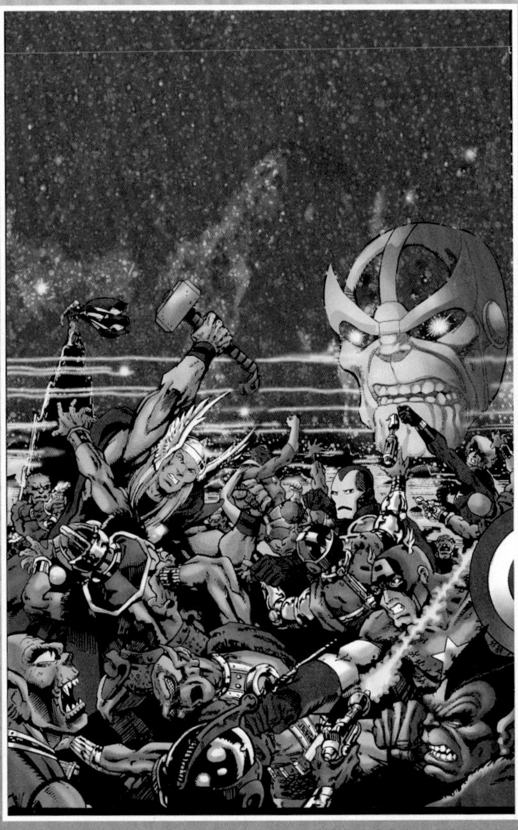

Essential Avengers Vol. 8 TPB back-cover art by Jim Starlin & Tom Smith

Essential Warlock Vol. 1 TPB back-cover art by Jim Starlin, Alan Weiss & Tom Smith

Avengers Vs. Thanos TPB cover
art by Jim Starlin & Thomas Mason

Recolored Gamora artwork from Avengers Vs. Thanos TPB, by John Byrne, Josef Rubinstein & Nelson Ribeiro

Warlock by Jim Starlin: The Complete Collection TPB
cover & back-cover art by Jim Starlin, Alan Weiss & Dean White